Adventu In Palmistry

By Catherine Kane

Illustrations by Tchipakkan

Foresight Publications
Wallingford, Ct.

Adventures in Palmistry ©Aug2010 by Catherine Kane

Illustrations by Tchipakkan – www.tchipakkan.com

ISBN 978-0-578-06413-0

Foresight Publications
Wallingford, Ct

This book is

dedicated to

my husband, Starwolf.

You are the Magick
and Adventure
and Song in my life…

<u>Acknowledgements</u>

They say that it takes a village to raise a child. That's true for books as well, so I'd like to take a moment to thank some of the members of my tribe.

To all of the folks whose palms have come before me over the last 40 years. Reading for you has been an honor.

To the members of the East Kingdom Soothsayer's guild, for being the first to test this knowledge in written form.

To Willow and Kat, for friendship, feedback and technical wizardry.

To Delilah, for her constant encouragement and faith in myself and my dreams.

To Tchipakkan, whose feedback and support kept me moving forwards.

And, to my wonderful husband, Starwolf. Without your patience, love and support, I would not be the palmist, author or woman that I am; and this book would not exist.

We're all in this together….

Table of Contents

Illustrations

<u>Hand Notes</u>

Hand notes are:

- useful tips,
- snippets of history,
- quotes,
- and other bits of interesting information about palmistry.

Watch for hand notes throughout this book.

<u>Hand Notes</u>

"The lines are not written into the human hands without reason,
they come from heavenly influences and man's own
individuality."

"De coelo et mundi causa

Aristotle

Introduction

So you'd like to learn to read palms, eh? Well, come into my tent.....

For 40 years, I've been reading palms, and loving it. To me, a palm reading that's well done does not only touch on the future, the past, money, and possibly the traditional "tall, dark stranger". It also serves to remind a client of her strengths, areas of need, and can empower her to live her best and brightest life. A good reading can be the fuel she needs to turn her life around, or know that she's on the right path, even if it seems a little bumpy right now...

Despite this, when I started to look around, I was startled to find that palmistry seemed at risk of becoming a dying art. There were many fine Tarot readers to be found, but few readers of palms. There were many people teaching Tarot, but not the art of the hand.

This didn't seem right, so I decided to start teaching as well as reading palms. When I did so, I discovered a curious thing. Student after student came into my class saying "I tried to learn from books, but couldn't manage it." By the end of class, these same students were able to read palms competently.

I later developed my live class into an online class, in order to teach people who couldn't reach me physically. Oddly enough, I found the same thing - a pattern of students who "couldn't learn from books", but were able to gain their skills through the course.

Now, there are lots of great books on palm reading out there (I learned many of my basic skills from books), but evidently, there's something that makes them hard for many students to follow. That's why this book is different.

As opposed to being in a standard book format, this book is strongly based on my on-line course. It's broken down into "bite-sized" chapters, in order to make the book more manageable, and less overwhelming. The diagrams are also broken down with a limited amount of information per picture to make them approachable.

There are 52 chapters in this book (originally designed to be one topic a week for a year to give students time to absorb each one before taking on the next). You can follow the original plan of one per week, or learn each lesson at your own pace as you prefer. I would recommend that you do them in order, as there is a fair amount of information that builds on previous information.

Regardless of why I wrote it, this book is here to meet your unique and special needs (because every one of us is different, unique, and special). Palmistry can put you in touch with your own inner wisdom and your natural psychic skills. It can make you aware of your own special talents, as well as things you need to work on. Palmistry can give you the information you need to make better choices in order to have a better life. It can empower you and give you the skills to empower other folks as well.

It's also a lot of fun; and a great way to meet people...

Welcome to your Adventures in Palmistry. May your journey of discovery be a joyful one.

Catherine Kane

Chapter 1

On Differences in Divination
and Why These Contradictions Work...

Let's start out by laying some groundwork, so that we're all on the same page.

From both my experience and that of the people I've talked to, psychic ability seems to be hard-wired into the human condition. While I can't say for certain that everybody's psychic (after all, I haven't met everybody yet), most of the people I've encountered seem to have one or more signs of innate ability, whether functioning consciously or unconsciously.

At that point, the different systems of divination seem less to be methods that are graven in stone, and more like frameworks that enable us to get in touch with what is in our heads, and our hearts, and our spirits. Different systems of divination (palmistry, tarot, tea leaves, etc.) may each have their own strengths and weaknesses, but they all boil down to different ways of touching the Wisdom that is within us and without us.

When it comes specifically to palmistry, you'll find a lot of books with a lot of different systems for reading palms out there. Many say different things. Some actually say *contradictory* things.

So what do we make of that?

That it all works (if you do the following)....

If you want to learn from books, I recommend that you chose a book that speaks to you. Learn from that, and then add to it with information from other books and other sources that don't contradict the first one

If you want to learn from this book (and I'm assuming you do, or you wouldn't be reading it), I recommend that you read it carefully, and try what I have to share with you. Take what resonates with you, and leave the rest, adding things from other sources that speak to you as you find them.

If you do this and listen to your own inner wisdom as to what is right when you do a reading, then you will find what you end up with will be amazingly effective...

No matter what book or system you chose...

I' m going to be teaching you the system that I've been working with for around 40 years. I look forwards to seeing how it evolves for you.

Chapter 2

On Ethical Readings and Finding the Right Words

Many people think that, because a person has active psychic abilities and is doing psychic readings, that person is somehow more "spiritual" and has higher standards of behavior than the average person.

While I haven't quite fallen into that error myself (I'm psychic, and I know how many "bad hair days" I have had personally), I've still been amazed throughout the years how many psychics there are who are "ethically challenged".

There are many psychics who are honestly trying to help people. They concentrate on empowering the people they're reading for –on giving you the information you need to make good decisions.

There are also many who aren't helpful. There are many who are just in it for the money, and will say or do whatever keeps that flowing, whether it's truthful or helpful, or not.

Worse yet, there are some psychics who are in it for the power, who enjoy playing head games and controlling people who come to them for help.

If you run into a psychic who makes you uneasy or that your inner wisdom tells you is bad news (such as those described above), I encourage you to excuse yourself to go take a phone call, leave and don't go back....

While I'm perfectly o.k. with people either charging money for readings or not doing so, dependant on the situation and their own values, I think the priority needs to be with two things.

First, providing the best, most accurate information that you are capable of, according to what's right for the client. (Standards of "right" include such things as age, comprehension, and what that client can handle at the moment.)

Second, to do this in a way that empowers people to make their own best decisions, as opposed to you, the reader, choosing for them.

I like to think that I'm in the business of putting the client in the driver's seat. I don't drive for them.

To do this, you need to first respect each client as being unique and worthy of respect.

I've heard many psychics say they "can't be bothered" with reading for giggly teen-aged girls or skeptics or (fill in the group of your choice here). It's like it's somehow beneath them to use their gift for people that they don't value; but to a teenager, the question of whether a boy likes her may be the most important thing in her life at this moment. To a skeptic, a glimpse that the world is slightly bigger and more magickal than he'd thought can change everything.

It's not our job to say whose concerns are important and whose are not. Just to serve.

You'll also run into people with different values than you. While some of these values may be leading to places the client might not want to end up (and it's your job to alert them to that), you do need to give that client the information on what's best for them, not how they can best follow your values. (For instance, I'm a very monogamous kind of woman who has on multiple occasions read for people with open relationships. That was the right thing for them at that time in their lives. I needed to read telling them what would work for them, even though it's not my way of doing things).

Different strokes for different folks.

One truly key issue feeding into ethical readings is the question of Free Will.

God, Goddess, the Universe or whomsoever you believe in has given you the ability to chose in life and, by choosing, have some control over who you are and where your life will go. Thus, you don't have just one future, but many possible ones, based on which choices you make; and any good reading tells you the statistically most likely future based on the direction you're heading now.

But you can change it....

In other words, if you keep doing things the way you're doing them, the reading tells you where you're going. If you don't want to go there, you need to see the exit ramp and get off. Change how you're doing things. If you change enough of the right things, who you are changes and the future changes to go with it!....

In palmistry, this means that, if you change the direction of your life enough, who you are changes and your future changes and (wait for it!), **YOUR HANDS CHANGE TO REFLECT IT!!!** (Sorry to shout but this is really important.) Your lines can change, the bumps called mounds can change, and even the shape of your hand can change.

This is crucial to know, not only for you but also for the people you read for.

Many people fear palmistry because they're afraid that I'll say something that they don't like and that they'll be stuck with it. When they find that Free Will makes palmistry a flexible roadmap as opposed to an inflexible portent of Doom, their fears vanish and they're ready to use it as it was meant to be used-as a guide to make better, informed choices.

I tend to explain this to each person I read for at the start of the reading, so they can use that reading to chose the best course for themselves.

Finally, people have differences about how much they're ready to hear, especially in regards to "challenging issues" (my term for what some readers call "bad stuff") and areas such as life expectancy.

Your job, as the reader, is to find the best way you can to help them hear as much of the truth you see in a way that they can hear and benefit from. To empower as opposed to overwhelm them. Because Free Will is an important factor in readings, what you see is likely but not inevitable, and you need to find your best way to help them to cross at the crosswalks, rather than be a deer in the headlights.

You also need to respect their right to take what they can but no more. A reading's not about you getting all this info out. It's about being there for the client and being sensitive to when they've gone as far as they can go.

For instance, there are signs that indicate depression in a palm. Because of Free Will, I interpret this as a vulnerability to depression, and talk to clients about making good choices, taking care to nurture themselves and avoiding dropping themselves into "the blues".

If they're already depressed, they'll admit it, but they still need this info to help get out of it. If they're on the brink, I avoid creating a self-fulfilling prophesy and pushing them into the pit of despair.

Now each of you will end up finding your own ways to interact with clients in a sensitive and respectful fashion, say sooth (tell the truth) in a way that your client can best hear and benefit from it, and have a style uniquely your own.

In addition to being a soothsayer, I'm a bard, an empath and a short, round, cute Teddy-Bearish woman. Because of this, I have phrases and stories that help people understand empowering concepts; tell jokes and act silly to help people hear challenging things; and really tune into my clients' energies to "hear" how best to reach them. I'll be glad to share my techniques with you, although you may find some work for you and some don't. At that point, please feel free to steal my "window trimming" as it works for you, or create your own.

I do, however, charge you, no matter your style, to be sure that you read in an ethical way, with your client's best interests in mind.

Empower them, and the World is a better place....

Chapter Three

Which Hand Do You Read?

One of the first questions people will ask you is "Which hand do you want?" or "Which hand do you read?" In the system I use, the answer is "Both!"

Traditionally, your non-dominant hand is the hand of the potential you were born with. This includes things such as genetic inheritance, the effects of our family's influence and the original path we started out on. It's what the Good Fairies brought to your christening (from a fairy tale standpoint as opposed to a religious ceremonial sense).

Your dominant hand is the hand of what you're doing with what you were given. It tells me more about who you are and where you're going now, so I'll focus more on it than the other hand but there are also a lot of things you can learn by comparing hands too, especially in certain areas (more of that anon...).

This is why your hands are different from each other.

Go on, check.

I'll wait......

How do you figure out which hand is dominant? For starters, I'll just ask "are you right or left handed?" The handedness is their hand dominance.

Sometimes, however, you'll get someone who's mixed dominance - who writes with their right hand but sews with their left and brushes their teeth with their elbow, etc. Many of these people are lefties who were forced to learn to write with their rights, due to archaic hand dominance bigotry, but some of them are people with true mixed hand dominance, due to injury or neurological issues.

When this happens, the first way to determine hand dominance is to ask "Which hand do you eat with?" (Never use writing as a test case as it is the most frequent activity where false handedness is enforced). Many times, this will give you the starting place you need.

If that doesn't work, the fall-back test is to place an item exactly in midline in front of the person (I use a goblet on my table that symbolizes water). Tell them briskly "Grab the goblet!" (Or aardvark or whatever you're using). Don't give them a chance to think about it and, if they start to ask for clarification, just repeat the question with emphasis. If you don't give them a chance to think, their automatic reactions will kick in and they'll grab with the dominant hand. (Always explain afterwards, so they don't feel like you're pushing them around).

It is possible to get someone with only one hand or hands that differ significantly from standard ones, due to injury, birth defects or other reasons. In these cases, hand dominance is based on what hand they're primarily using, regardless of what hand dominance they started out with. For all other variations, you take a deep breath, connect with Spirit, care about your client and do the best you can.

One of the most challenging readings I ever did was for a woman whose mother had taken Thalidomide while pregnant with her. Both of her hands were markedly different from what I was used to (her more whole hand had only half a palm, a thumb and two webbed fingers). This significantly affected the landmarks you'll be learning, but, despite this, I ended up giving her a reading that she found surprising and accurate.

If I could do that, I feel sure that you can, too.

When reading palms, you'll focus primarily on the dominant hand, in order to give the current forecast. Looking at both hands to compare them is particularly useful in certain areas, however.

For instance, someone who has poor health indicators in her non-dominant hand but better ones in the dominant is someone who started with potential health risks, but has overcome them due to good choices on her part.

(Go on! Give her a pat on the back! She's earned it!)

Those potential health problems could be due to elements such as genetics, or things her family taught her about things affecting her health, such as diet or exercise. Both Nature and Nurture make their appearance in the non-dominant hand.

As another example, someone whose non-dominant hand has a large mound of Apollo (arts and sciences) but a tiny little "boomp" in their dominant hand is someone who has a natural ability for an art or science but isn't using it yet.

I'll be going into this more in the specific areas, but I hope this gives you the basic understanding of how this works.

One other related thing to think about in reading palms is "How do you hold the hand?" It's been my experience that most people, when offering you their palm to read, will present it with the fingers tense and stretched out as far back as they can go, particularly if it is their first time having their palms read.

This doesn't work real well.

Look at your own palm. Stretch the fingers out rigidly, and then let them relax into a normal cupped position. What differences do you see?

If you're like most folks, you'll see that the lines, particularly the lighter ones, distort or disappear when you tense those fingers. We don't want that.

The ideal position of a palm for reading is in a naturally relaxed, slightly cupped position, with the thumb in neutral (neither crossing the palm nor sticking out at an angle but tucked naturally over the border of the palm).

This is not the position that most people will initially give you. How do you get them there? You can say "Relax" but I find that makes most people tenser (go figure!). I tend to smile at them, take one finger, then shriek "R-E-L-A-X!!!" in a loud, silly voice while shaking the hand briskly .Since I'm small, round and cute, they tend to

startle, crack up and relax for me, however, if you're a 6'3" Barbarian, you might
need to find an alternative technique.....

Now we're ready to go....

Chapter 4

On Reading the Individual Script of the Hand

In palmistry, each landmark, such as a line or mound, stands for one or more individual characteristics. For example, the heart line deals with love, romance and other emotional issues. The mound of Jupiter stands for leadership, self-esteem and other such factors (Once again, more of this anon...)

In reading lines, the darker or deeper a line is, the more of the characteristic indicated by that line is possessed by the person attached to the hand.

So what's a dark line? What's a light line? How does one figure that out?

First and foremost, you never compare one person's lines to another person's to determine whether a line is dark or light. Just as one person's handwriting can be very different from another's, the definition of dark or light lines in their hands can also be very different (I like to say "one person's lines can be written in little-old-lady copper print script, and another person's drawn in with a Magic Marker" ....)

Take the person's hand in yours. Be sure it's held in a relaxed, natural, cupped position (as discussed in chapter 3), so that all of the lines are at their best, and no lighter ones are distorted or obscured.

Then compare that person's lines to each other.

The lines qualify as lighter or darker based on how they appear in the overall context of both of the client's hands. There's no checking your neighbor, no trying to keep up with the Joneses. Just how each aspect of yourself meshes with the rest of you.

It's kinda Zen, in its way.

Some people will have very busy hands with lots of little lines (oddly enough, they frequently seem embarrassed by this). Some will have simpler hands with fewer but boldly drawn lines.

And every variation between.

And...it's all good. Because every person is unique and special and every palm reflects this.

People will sometimes laugh nervously and ask if they've got an interesting palm. I always say yes, because they all are.

Just like the people attached to them.

Figure 1 - Markings

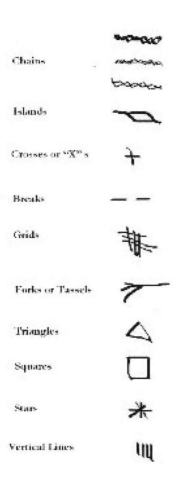

Chains

Islands

Crosses or "X" s

Breaks

Grids

Forks or Tassels

Triangles

Squares

Stars

Vertical Lines

Figure 1 – Markings

<u>Hand Notes</u>

Many times, you'll get folks who say they're scared of getting a palm reading. They say that they're afraid to know what lies ahead of them in the future.

This is because these people are afraid that if you see something they don't like and tell them about it, they're stuck with it. There's an unconscious superstition that if they don't hear about it, nothing bad will happen.

This makes sense when you realize that most of them don't know about the effects of Free Will on the palm....

Tell them about Free Will. Tell them free of charge. Tell them that, whether they get a reading or not, they don't need to fear readings and you want to give them the information they need to let go of this fear.

Clearing unnecessary fear out of the world makes it a better place

Interestingly enough, once you can show people that they do not need to fear the future and what a good reading can tell them, many of these people will actually get a reading with you.

Chapter 5

Markings in Palmistry - the Building Blocks of a Reading I- the Markings of Challenge

In palmistry, there are certain markings that can appear throughout the palm. Each mark stands for a certain kind of phenomenon or experience.

The palm is made up of landmarks, such as lines or mounds (those would be the "boomps"). Each landmark stands for a different characteristic, such as love, intelligence or creativity; and a marking on that landmark indicates ways in which that characteristic is expressed. For instance, a marking indicating a gift appearing on the landmark that stands for the Arts and Sciences would indicate a natural gift in an Art or a Science.

Where markings appear, it's a good idea to compare both hands to gain more information. As you may recall from a previous chapter, the non-dominant hand is the hand of the potential you were born with and the dominant hand is the hand of what you're doing with it.

Taking that into consideration, if you had a mark indicating that gift on the mound of Arts and Sciences in your non-dominant hand but not in your dominant, it'd indicate you had a natural gift but the kind of life you're currently living works against that gift so significantly that you can't access it.

If on the other hand, you had that gift in the dominant hand but not in your non-dominant, it would indicate that you'd developed great skills through your own hard work. (Good for you!)

Some lines have a timeline (indicating different periods in your life). Some lines do not. If a marking appears on a line with a timeline, the effect of the marking is felt for the part of the life covered by the marking. If it appears on a line without a timeline or on a mound, it simply indicates how the characteristic covered by that landmark is currently expressed.

I'm going to start by reviewing the basic meanings of the markings that you'll be looking for throughout the palm. Later on, as we go through the various landmarks, I'll give additional examples of how these markings affect those landmarks, but, overall, once you know the meanings of the markings, combining their meanings with the meanings of the landmarks is largely common sense. To make things clearer as we go over the meaning of these markings, you'll want to refer to Figure 1 "Markings"

In this chapter, we'll start with the more negative or challenging markings; and in the next chapter, we'll have the more positive ones for dessert...

Chains - Chains are not exclusively little round links. They can also be series of diamonds, ovals, triangles, etc. Just think of anything that looks like it comes off one of those "chains-by-the-yard" set-ups you see to make custom necklaces in jewelry stores or on carts at the mall.

Chains stand for "disturbances".

Islands - Islands are places where the line splits in two and comes together again, forming an enclosed area. Islands stand for "confinement". This can be literal confinement (such as jail or being homebound by a serious illness) but frequently they appear to indicate feeling "stuck", "trapped", "spinning your wheels" or "in a rut".

Unhappy marriages, dead end jobs and lack of progress towards your true dreams all hang out on islands.

Although this seems bad, it isn't always. Sometimes, the "stuck" period of an island is the germination period that something wonderful needs to grow.

If you see an island, it can be empowering to your querant to realize that "island time" may not be wasted time, but rather time for their efforts to come to fruition. It can likewise be helpful to know how long the "island" will last.

You can also empower them by reminding them that their palm tells what happens if they continue to do what they're doing-if they don't want to stay confined, they need to use that free will and do something different to change that path. (We see the exit ramp, we get off!...)

Crosses- Crosses can look like crosses or "X"s.

If they are between the head and heart lines, they are **Mystic Crosses**, signs of particular psychic abilities we'll be discussing much further along in this book. In all other positions, they stand for "opposition".

When looking at crosses, if the more horizontal arm of the cross is darker/more prominent, whatever opposes you is winning. If the vertical arm is darker, you are winning. (Many times there will not be a definite vertical or horizontal arm, so you must decide which arm is the most aligned in that way.)

Breaks - Breaks stand for "a major change in direction". In many cases, they indicate a period in time where the options are so wide open that there is not one most likely life path. (I tend to think "Magic 8 ball says "Ask Again Later".).There will not be a visible line/path until you make more choices with your free will that send you down one path or another. From personal experience, once you do so, the line will fill in.

Grids- Look kind of like screen door material. These also mean "opposition". Sometimes they mean more severe opposition or from multiple sources.

Finally,

Tassels/Forks- Points at the end of lines where the line splits into several branches.

There are a few places in the hand where tassels or forks are neutral or even good things, and I'll discuss them as we get there. In most cases, they mean "Deterioration or dispersion" of the element. For example, a tassel on the line dealing with emotions tends to belong to someone with a lot of "drama", who has emotional tizzies/tantrums/etc. all over the place.

That seems like enough for now. In the next chapter, we'll tackle the positive markings

Chapter 6

Markings in Palmistry-the Building Blocks of a Reading II - The Markings of Joy

Last time, we went over the markings indicating challenges or negative things.

Whew! Glad that's over!

Now we get to go over the more positive markings, the ones which are always a pleasure to see in a palm. Turn your attention once again to Figure 1, "Markings".

Triangles- Triangles are "gifts". Dependant on where they occur and what else is happening in the palm, they can be literal gifts or they can be periods of good fortune. These are times when things you normally have to work your fanny off for just drop into your lap; or things that normally would be too good to be true, in this case aren't.

The image I like is that "the peeled grape....drops off the vine into your open mouth....and it is sweet......"

Another good term for a triangle is "Grace".

Squares- Squares are "protection". This can be protection from this side of the veil or the other side. Often, when you have a break in a line (remember from last chapter-this means a change in direction...), you'll see a square around the break, indicating experiencing significant change but being protected while you do it.

Stars- Stars are not pentacle- type stars (such as seen in palms in werewolf movies). In this context, a star is an asterix.

Stars stand for "unusual events". They are usually fortunate, except if they occur on the life line (where they mean "crisis").

Finally,

A series of vertical little lines- In most positions, they stand for "unusual grit (that's true grit, folks!) or determination".

If you see these kind of lines on the mound of Mercury (which we'll be visiting much later in this book), they're called "Healer's Stigmata". They tend to appear in the hands of people who either are healers or have a natural talent for the healer's path. This includes both mainstream medical folk and alternative healing practitioners, including energy healers. It also includes people in related healing and human services fields, such as E.M.T.s, therapists, counselors, pharmacists and certain kinds of police and firemen (think Officer Friendly).

As noted in the previous section on markings, remember to compare hands. A mark in the non-dominant hand but not in the dominant means potential as yet unrealized. In the dominant hand but not the non-dominant means gifts achieved through your own hard work, beyond your own natural gifts.

It doesn't seem fair that there are a lot fewer positive markings than negative ones.

Don't worry, though. We've got a lot more good things coming up in the palm.

Figure 2 - Life Line, Head Line, Heart Line

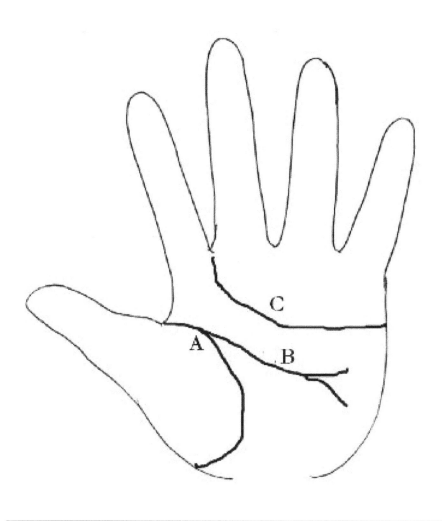

Figure 2 – Life Line, Head Line, Heart Line

<u>Hand Notes</u>

There's a lot of information in a palm.

When doing a full reading, it's a good idea to ask if your querant has a specific question or area of concern, or if she would prefer a general reading.

In a general reading, a querant's head can get filled to the top by the end of the reading, and she may not absorb everything. Because of this, if she has something she specifically wants to know about, it's a good idea to address this first

Once her specific interests are addressed, now you can go on and do the rest of the reading if your querant wants more information

Chapter 7-

Life Line I
-the Time of Your Life

The life line is the (hopefully) long line that circles around the base of your thumb (for location specifics, please look at Figure 2, "Life Line, Head Line, Heart Line". The life line is labeled "A".) It covers the big picture of your life, giving the overall journey from cradle to grave. It points out major occurrences, life expectancy and personal energy, amongst other things.

To avoid confusion while looking at this line, please note that the life line curves around the base of the thumb, as pictured in the diagram, and the major differences between life lines are how far they extend, how light or deep they are, and any markings found upon the life line.

There is another line (the Fate line) that starts in the middle of the bottom of the palm and goes upwards to end under the middle finger. This line will sometimes brush against or meld with the life line. (More details when we get to this line in later chapters.) If this happens, it can sometimes confuse a beginning reader by looking like the life line dives straight down and ends in the palm's center. Please disregard that and follow the natural curve of the life line as described and illustrated.

In the system I use, only some of the lines have time lines (enabling you to view the progression of life on the issue covered by that line, and to check out what's slated to happen when.) The life line (not surprisingly) is one of these. Here's how to read the time line on your life line.

The birth end of the life line is above the thumb, at the point on your handout marked "A". You follow the line around as it circles the thumb until it ends (which would be death or your next incarnation, dependant on your viewpoint on the hereafter).

The first thing you'll be looking at is how long a life will this person have; followed by what's happening when in his life....

If you place the thumb of your free hand (the one not supporting your querant's hand) on the heel of your client's hand on the bottom of the mound at the base of the thumb, and feel about a bit, you'll find a bone that sticks up a bit (one of your carpals, for those of you who like medical terminology).

The point where the lifeline crosses this bone is age "80"

That would make the point on the life line that is halfway between the birth end and that bone age "40".

And 1/4 of the way from birth to that bone age "20".

And so forth.

Many times, you'll find a life line extending beyond that point (Or at least I find this happens often. Maybe it's just that all the long-lived folk come sit with me. Oh well, you got to go by what you know...) Sometimes the line even wraps onto the back of the palm (a very long life).

Life expectancy is one of the two things that frequently are scary to querants. You're going to need to know it for yourself because you'll need it to estimate times on the other lines, but (from my experience) it's a good idea to ask your subject if they want to know this before you tell them.

If they say no, giggle nervously or make a frightened face, it's best to either skip it, tell them that it's a long life line (if that's true, of course) or remind them about the free will information that you've already given them - that they can always change things ("Oat bran and exercise can increase this! Walking in front of a bus puts new lines on your hand and voids the warrantee!")

Sometimes (relatively rarely), you'll get someone with a short life line, or (even worse) someone with a short life line that ends soon and who knows what this means. (This happened once to me-very challenging.) If this is the case, it is unethical to:

1) Say "you will die soon!";

2) Gasp and freak out;

3) Return their money and order them out of your tent; or

4) Indulge in any other such behavior

(And yes, I've heard stories of readings like this).

Remember, they've got free will...which means no matter how close the end appears or how dire the line looks, they have a chance to change it.

In such times, you owe it to your querants to keep it together and empower them to do their best to overcome it, rather than push them into the despair that can make them stop trying.

You do not say "you'll die in 3 years."

You say "in 3 years, I see a very crucial time in your life where it's very important for you to take every precaution to guard your health and safety". You remind them of their free will, and that, since their palm indicates a less desirable result if they keep doing things the way they have, they might want to choose to change direction. You help them to laugh and relax so they can actually deal with their challenge.

The life line is like the course of a ship. When there is an obstacle in a ship's course that is far away, a minor course correction is needed to avoid it. If closer to, you'll need a more major course correction. With free will, there's always a chance and you want to give them that chance.

One other odd phenomenon I've run across is people who, when you tell them that there's a good, long life ahead of them, make a face, say something disgusted or otherwise indicate they don't want to live a long time (not suicidal, just not happy with the idea of getting old).

My impulse when I get one of these folks is to shake them

vigorously and tell them "If you don't like the way your life is, change it to something you do like, but be happy you've got lots of time to choose!"

The shaking (of course) is unethical, as is interfering with their free will to choose to be miserable. I usually therefore take a deep breath and look for a tactful way to slip the idea in that they are also free to chose a joyful way of life.....

And that it's not a bad thing to have plenty of time to find and live that joy.....

More on the life line is coming your way soon....

Chapter 8-

Life Line II
-As Time Goes By

In the last chapter, we looked at the life line's time line and the elements surrounding the issue of life expectancy. This chapter, let's get into some other aspects of the life line.

When you start reading the life line, you look at life expectancy first (both to find out this information for the client, and to have that knowledge for yourself to use while estimating time lines on other lines). You ask the client whether they want to know their life expectancy. What you tell them depends on your clients' reaction and what it tells you about how much they're willing and able to hear about this.

(While life expectancy is one of the most frequently touchy issues in a palm, this question of how much to tell and in what way is one that comes up repeatedly and separates a good reader from a bad one. In early times, a psychic was called a "soothsayer" because it was his job to "say sooth"/tell the truth. It is your job to tell your client the truth. You must also respect the client's right to deal with things as best they can and tell the truth, both in quantity and quality, in a way that your client can best hear and benefit from it....)

The next thing to look at is what's going on in and around the present. Ask how old your querant is. (I always ask "if you don't mind..." because, while people are less touchy about their ages than they used to be, you'll still occasionally run into someone who doesn't like to tell their age. If so, so be it.)

Using that "80 year" mark, estimate back to find the point on the life line that falls around now......

Here's the point where you start looking for those markings you learned about in Chapters 5 and 6 (you knew you'd use them sooner or later, right? ...). Let's lay out some examples:

Is there an island on the "now" part of the line? That's a period when the client is confined/trapped/stuck/spinning their wheels. They need to have this stasis acknowledged, know how long this will last if they keep doing things the way they have been, and be reminded that free will means they can break free of their stasis by changing the things that they're doing.

It's also good to note that this kind of confinement or rut can sometimes be the germination period needed to plant good things that'll sprout later on. It's not necessarily wasted time.

Is there a triangle here? This is a period of gift(s) from the Universe or Grace (and always fun to report). The querant needs to be alerted to watch for the gifts from the divine so that he or she is ready to accept or take advantage of them.

What about a fork? On a lifeline, a fork frequently means a time with two equally likely future paths pending. If it's a long one, the client may be trying to live both futures (not a double life, but rather vacillating between both, or maybe having both)

That's fine, but usually that person will have to choose one or the other path sooner or later in order to fully live their life rather than just survive it. They need a bit of reassurance, and the reminder to look at their choices and consciously choose, rather than drift where the current takes them or burn out trying to do both...

What if there are no special markings (positive or negative) at this point in the line? Well, that's a life that's on track and under full steam, moving forwards. The kind of life that most of us experience a majority of the time.

It's useful not only to look at what's going on now, but also the time span individual markings cover. For example, a tiny triangle can be a miraculous period of three months whereas a long island can be a seven year dry spell. Getting the time spans is tricky at first, but the more you practice, the better you'll get at it.

I find most people are usually accepting of the term "approximately".

It's usually most useful to focus on what's happening "now", but it can also serve a client to report things coming up in the future so they can be prepared for them or else shift to avoid them. For instance, I'll frequently see forks (choices) or breaks (major changes in direction) between 65 and 75 (around the retirement years-imagine that!) Often these clear after a short time and change to a single line that continues on. It's good in such cases to alert your querant to a period of change and upheaval but let them know it'll come out ok.

You could find just about any of the markings on the life line and, given these examples, I'm sure that you can extrapolate what the various markings indicate when they turn up on this line. A triangle at 35, a 7 year island starting at age 20- try it yourself and see what stories the life line can tell you.

One other interesting thing about the life line is that it indicates energy/"chi"/vital force. The deeper your life line is at any point in time, the more energy you have.

Your chi level may vary throughout your life. Often the line is lighter (indicating less energy) towards the end of life but I have seen folks where their energy increases (they retire and have more time to exercise, perhaps?).

You can also have periods during your life where you get drained. Not a bad thing to cue people into that and remind them to take care of themselves.

The energy indicated by the life line can be distinct from or linked to health issues (health issues have their own line that we'll get to later on).

Sometimes you'll see people with a double or even a triple life line. This would be a second or third line that parallels the first one for part or all of their life (as opposed to a fork).

During this period, these people have the energy of two or more people. They are frequently confused why other folks can't keep up with them (I like to remind them that this is because they have the super powers and we don't). If the double line only lasts for part of their life (a feature frequently seen) you need to cue them to enjoy it as an extra gift they've received but to remember to be kind to us mortals because they'll be one of us soon enough....

This concludes our introductory tour of the life line. Next stop, the head line!

Chapter Nine

Head Line I-
Get Your Head in the Game

Having done a basic overview of the life line, it's time to move on to the next line - the head line.

When you look at a palm, there are usually two lines that run horizontally across the palm. The head line is the lower of these two lines and usually (but not always) starts out by overlapping the birth end of the life line. (For a visual representation, please consult Figure 2, "Life Line, Head Line, Heart Line" for the basic location of this line. It is line "B").

The head line stands for intelligence, intellect, logic, reasoning, education, creativity, organization, smarts - in short, all the logical left-brained aspects of the person. The length, depth and slope of this line and what markings are on it (there's those markings again!.....) indicate how much of a "thinking" person one is, and the kind of thinker you are.

If your head line goes straight and level across your palm, you tend to be a more logical, linear thinker. You sort out problems from an organized, linear pattern (going first to "A", then "B", then "C", and so forth) You also tend to be organized. (It may be a system of organization that no one else gets, but it works perfectly for you.) Barring other contradictory factors, you tend to have good judgment and reasonably good willpower. (This can be undermined by other aspects of the palm.)

If this line is completely level across the palm, you're probably a brilliant analyst with an almost scientific type of mind (regardless of what topic interests you most) but you can get so serious that you forget to have fun. You need someone to remind you to stop and smell the roses....

If your head line slants gently downwards, you tend to be a

more creative, non-linear type of thinker. You solve problems in ways
no one else would even think of (ex: you leap from "A", to "12", to
"hydrangea", etc., then end up at an answer with no logical trail of
deduction). You frequently come up with new ideas out of nowhere.
You're an intuitive thinker. Here, "intuitive" does not refer to
"psychic", although you may be that as well, but more to thinking by
leaps of inspiration. I like to say "You not only think outside the box,
you think outside the entire toy store!" The more the head line slopes,
the more of a creative thinker you are.

Both types of thinking style enjoy thinking games, if they have
the signs of an active brain. The folks with level head lines tend to
enjoy logic problems, like Sudoku and those stories that end with"
which brother owns the moose?" where they can reason things out.
The ones with slanted head lines tend to enjoy murder mysteries and
riddles, where they can form a theory, then find the logic that supports
it (or not).

If a head line slopes severely downwards, heading towards the
heel of the hand, this type of line belongs to a person who is still
wildly creative but also either depressed or else has an above average
vulnerability to depression. (I tend to think of Vincent Van Gogh.)
This can be either a result of body chemistry (some folks just have a
genetic pre-disposition to depression) or to their circumstances. To
get a clearer take on this, check their non-dominant hand as well. If
the slope appears only in the dominant hand, it's probably situational.
If it's in both hands, it tends to come from the family, whether due to
genetics/body chemistry or the way that family raised him.

Why's that important? Well, a situational depression is often
an appropriate response to a current situation. This situation can
change or be changed, and the depression then passes. It can therefore
be easier to change than one that's based in altered body chemistry.
(Please note - a situational depression that lasts long enough can alter
body chemistry leading to the more permanent type, so it's still
important to take care of oneself.)

This is one of those areas where you need to take extra care with what you say and how you say it. If your querant is struggling with managing depression, saying something insensitive like "You're depressed" can make you look impressive but tip the querant onto the downhill slide into depression. You need to find a way to cue this person that it's important to do what they need to do to stay off that slide (and what to do is different for everyone. Once you remind them, most know what's going to work for them, but some may need additional input). You need to do this in a way that's non-scary, respectful, sensitive and empowering for them. Each of you may have to take a different slant on this.

I'm going to share the "story" with you that I use with folks in this situation. Because I'm short, round and built like a teddy bear, I can get away with jokes; because I'm a bard, telling stories works for me to get points across in a non-threatening manner; because I'm an empath (psychic on an emotional level), I can help folks feel safe while we face the monster in the closet together. This "story" may work for you too, or you may have to find a different way to address this issue.

If I see the depression type head line, I stop, take an unobtrusive deep breath and center myself. I'm going to have to be calm, charming and slightly flirtatious (in a non-sexual way) to make this work.

Then I say, "I see by your head line that "the Blues" wants to be your friend...and if you let it, "the Blues" will come and stay with you, and eat all the food in your fridge and use all your bath towels, and be a very bad house guest. So your job, when "the Blues" comes down your street and knocks on your door, (because it knows where you live), is to lock the door, and say (in a bad accent) "There is no one here by that name, Senor!", and **don't let him in!!!**."

Then I make eye contact and say, in a gentler, less story-telling voice, "By "the Blues", of course, you know I mean depression."

At this point, the querant is relaxed (and frequently laughing) and will either say they're depressed or that they've struggled with it throughout their life. We then talk about prioritizing the things that put their head in a good space, if they're not currently there. If they are in a better space, we talk about the things that keep them there. I always emphasize that, if they take responsibility for their own mental well-being, they've got a better shot at a good life than if they hope that life will make them happy.

One phrase I like is, "It's easier to stay out of a tiger trap than to get out once you've fallen in (especially if there's already a tiger in there!)"

Most of them already know what they need to do to stay in the happy space as opposed to the tiger trap. They just need a reminder that that is a priority, too; or permission to take good care of themselves; or the idea that nurturing themselves is a **good** thing, not a selfish one.

If this "story" works for you, feel free to co-opt some or all of it (I'll consider it my gift to you and the folks living with depression in the world). If not, I recommend you think about how you'll respond in a caring, empowering manner when this issue comes up (it will- depression's a common element seen in readings)

And, by the by, if you run into someone who's got a depressive slope in their non-dominant hand but not their dominant, that means they've made such good choices that, for the most part, they've overcome depression.

Praise 'em big (they've earned it!) but caution them to continue to make good choices so they don't overextend themselves and become vulnerable again.

Chapter Ten

Head Line II-
Head Lines, Head Lines, Read All About It!

All right, then! Last chapter, we started looking at the head line and how it's degree of downwards slant affects the kind of thinker your querant is. This chapter, let's look at some other aspects of the head line and some examples of what some of those markings on it can mean. (Here come those useful markings, again!)

In the system that I use, there is no time line on the head or heart lines. In other words, you're not ignorant now and brilliant later on. (You may well be but the palm will change to reflect that). It just indicates the intellectual (or, for the heart line, emotional) nature that you're currently living.

First, let's look at the script of the head line. The longer and darker a head line is, the more of a thinker that person is.

If it's long and dark, give him a pat on the back for how brainy he is!

If the line is long and light, usually that's a person who has wonderful brains but doesn't use them. I'll usually try to be tactful about this, but sometimes I'll just say it. (I see this a lot in teenagers, especially young, teenaged girls. I'll tell them they have great brains but that they don't use them as much as they could. They and their friends usually crack up hysterically and really enjoy this. Then we talk about ways that it can be fun to let your brains come out and play.) Get a feel for your client to chose which approach will work better for him.

If it's short and dark, that's someone who makes the most of what he's got but isn't particularly analytical. Give him praise for doing his best. Many times, this kind of person may function more from an emotional basis and have a more developed heart line instead.

If it's short and light, be polite. Move on and find something else to focus on.....

Forks at the end of lines are usually wasted energy and are a negative sign. Not at the end of a head line! A fork at the end of your head line is called a "Writer's Fork" and it appears on the palm of someone who either writes or has a natural ability to write. In other words, a special gift for playing with words. Most times, people will blush and acknowledge it when you tell them this. (Many of the folks with writers' forks write poetry in secret.) It's still important to say it, because many times, they think of it as "that little thing I like to do" as opposed to a true talent, and hearing it from someone else can cause them to look at it in a whole different way....

Occasionally, you'll get someone who's surprised to hear this; or who even thinks of himself as hating to write. This is often someone who associates writing with laborious school assignments. Remind him that it's very different to write about things you like because you want to. Watch the interesting expressions that flow across his face at this point.....

You may have opened up a whole new part of the world to him.....

Forks in the body of the head line indicate someone who has a problem making up his mind. This can be indecision or, otherwise, the ability to see all sides of an issue so much that it becomes hard to choose. Talk to him about weighing his options, choosing and living with his choice without regret.

Breaks in a head line tend to indicate someone having problems with "spacing out". Talk to this person about focus.

Chains in a head line stand for thoughts that go around and around. (I think of this as "squirrel cage" thinking.) Talk to him about breaking out of mental ruts that are traps for him.

Triangles would be special mental gifts. (I love seeing triangles!).

These are some examples of what those markings can mean when you see them on the head line. Think about the other markings you already know about. What do you think that they would mean in the context of intelligence and thought?

It's also worth noting that judgment is located in the head line; not the negative type of judgment (which involves turning up your nose at people or things that are different from you) but rather the positive type of judgment that helps you make good choices and avoid doing foolish things.

Head Notes

Often a querant may arrive at your table with a group of people. This is particularly likely at fairs, benefits and other public events. At this point, the question arises whether you are reading for one person privately, or with a group of people looking on.

My experience is that some folks like to be read with their friends and family listening. These other folks help them to remember things from the reading, and make the experience more fun.

Other people prefer for the reading to be private. They'll send their entourage off to shop.

I'm not shy reading for groups. Because of this, I find that the best option in these circumstances is to ask the querant what she prefers.

Chapter Eleven

Life Line/Head Line-
Childhood and the Changeling

Now we're going to examine the special aspects of life line and head line working together.

In most palms, the life line (at the birth end) and the head line start together as one, separating after varying lengths of space/time. That overlap indicates childhood and the time when the two lines separate indicates the time where the querant separated from his family, whether physically moving out or emotionally becoming independent, and started living his own life as an individual.

In most palms, this section of the life line/head line will have chains/feathers/breaks and all manner of less than ideal markings. That's because childhood, while being great, is also a big struggle to learn the rules of life and how one is a part of it. It can be a lot of fun, but it's not idyllic and it comes with its own load of struggles, "alarums and excursions" (and not the kind that come with a picnic lunch and a trip to the gift shop).

The length of the connection between life line and head line not only indicates the time one spent as a part of a family, but also, to a certain extent, the influence your family has on you to this day. This influence can be either for good or ill. (For instance, if you went into thrash metal just to make a statement to your conservative parents, they still hold a good deal of influence over you. You're basing your behavior and your life on what they think.)

If the connection is short, you probably have minimal contact with your family and are not very influenced by them. If it's long, you are tight with your family and, in effect, carry them about with you in your head.

Whether this is for good or ill depends on your family and on you.

In certain palms, the life line and head line are totally discrete and do not touch at all. Per most references and other palmists I've spoken to, this is extremely rare. Despite this, people like this seem to flock to my table in the hundreds. I'm not sure whether this is because this palm variation is not as truly rare as authorities think or whether my style is comfortable for folks of this type, drawing them all to me......

The person with separate life and head lines is like a stranger in his own family. It's like someone swapped the babies at the hospital. Like his family is marching to John Phillip Sousa while he is dancing the lambada. His family may love him - or they may not; but they are never going to understand him. This is a situation that comes with a whole heap of its own dirty laundry.

I think of these folks as "Changelings". For any of you who may not have heard this term, it is a story that goes back to early times (medieval or earlier) where the Fair Folk (elves or other such enchanted personages) would steal a human baby and leave a changeling in its place...

When dealing with this kind of changeling, you have a fair bit of ground to cover.

First, you need to note how they are very different from their families and that **this is perfectly o.k.** Some changelings have come to terms with their differences, but many go through life feeling that there's something wrong with them and trying frantically to fit into a mold that they were never created to fit. For healing and empowerment, a changeling needs to know that it's fine to be who he is as opposed to someone else (I like to say "The ugly duckling was a terrible duckling because he was really a beautiful swan, and you also make a pretty poor duckling...")

Second, it's important to note that his family may or may not love him, but they're probably never (ever, ever) going to truly understand him. For your querant to be happy with his life, he needs to let go of something that is unlikely to impossible, such as true understanding in this case.

Third, it's good to note that the family may often pressure the changeling to do what they think is good for him, something which is often completely wrong for a changeling. Now this can be due to manipulation or control issues, but it may also be due to their not "getting" the changeling. It's usually a mentally healthier choice to assume such pressure is due to ignorance, rather than nastiness, unless there's proof of such cussedness.

Finally, in such circumstances, for a changeling to be happy himself (whether it makes the family happy or not), he needs to be able to say "Well, thanks for thinking of me and caring, but I've got my own song to sing/my own dance to dance/my own path to walk".

Caring for people does not mean you need to deny your own calling to fit into their vision of you.

A changeling needs to follow his own special road, and he may need support from your reading to confirm this - that's it's more than o.k. to be perfectly, uniquely, beautifully himself and no one else.

Well, this completes this chapter. On to the next!

<u>Hand Notes</u>

"He sealeth up the hand of every man; that all men may know his work."

Job 37:7

The Bible

Chapter Twelve

Heart Line I-
Owner of a Lonely Heart...

On to our next line - the heart line. The heart line is the upper of the two major horizontal lines crossing the palm. (See Figure 2 "Head Line, Heart Line". The heart line is labeled "C".)

The heart line stands for emotions/intuition/feelings/all of the non-linear, non-logical aspects of personality that are not covered by the head line. Like the head line, it does not have a time line but rather references the emotional energy you currently put out.

Let's start with the length of your heart line. Your heart line starts on the pinkie side of the palm and goes across it towards the side with the index finger.

To judge the length, picture an imaginary vertical line that starts between your index and middle fingers and drops straight downwards. This is your reference mark. A heart line that reaches this line is average. A heart line that stops before it is short. A heart line that passes beyond it is long.

A person who has a short heart line tends to be shy or withdrawn. (I like the term "a private person") She has a hard time trusting people and trusting the Universe to be a decent place overall. She tends to conceal her true vulnerable nature behind a mask, or armor plate, or any other option that protects her from the risk of being hurt by others.

Now, it's perfectly o.k. to be more reserved. Not everyone has to be wildly outgoing. Unfortunately, these protections come with a price tag and it's your job to let your client know that, by gaining safety in this way, she loses other things in life. She needs to know this so she can make good, conscious choices.

The person who can't trust other people keeps everyone at arm's length. This means that she cannot have close relationships –

that means friendship and family and love and all of the close human things.

The person who can't trust the Universe to be overall o.k. becomes afraid- afraid to risk, afraid to dare, afraid to dream, afraid to do the deeds that might be most glorious in her. I don't say things never go wrong in life, but to expect it as the norm prevents you from living your best life possible.

The person who hides behind a mask or armor protects her vulnerable parts but also denies people the chance to get to know and love and respect her true self. There are people for every one of us who are worthy of the honor of knowing our true selves; and who would give us such magnificent love and respect in return if we let them. If we close them out, we'll never know.

Furthermore, by disguising her true self, such a person usually denies that self. This hurts her self-esteem and leaves her disempowered and doubting herself.

When you see someone with a short heart line, you need to acknowledge that her choice is a valid one, but let her know that it comes at a price. Since she has free will, it's up to her to choose if and when she might want to come out of her shell (using the good judgment in the head line to choose the right people to do it to). It's up to you to let her know what her present choices cost...

When you see a short heart line, check the non-dominant hand. If that one's longer, it means that person started out more open, but has gone through some hurtful event which has caused her to close down and put the armor on her heart. If they're both short, this person is naturally reserved and has always been so.

Why does that matter? Well, the person who's withdrawn because she's been hurt will find it easier (comparatively) to open up. She's been in an open-hearted life before and knows what it feels like. The person who's always been an introvert has a harder task to accomplish, if she chooses to open her heart, because she's setting out into unfamiliar territory....

Let me be clear here- I'm not saying that being introverted or shy is bad. I'm just saying that it has a price, a price that most of us would not want to pay if we knew it was part of the package. Whether to open up at all, how much to open up, how fast to open up and when - that's all up to the client. As an ethical reader, you need to respect her decisions for her own life. It's just up to you to give her the information she needs to make informed choices

<u>Hand Notes</u>

Many times, readings are fun.

Sometimes they're not. Sometimes issues come up in a reading that are challenging, sad, traumatic or frustrating.

It's your job to help your querant get through this.

One thing I've found that helps is having a piece of rose quartz on the table. Rose quartz puts out a friendly, comforting healing energy that can be very helpful in challenging situations.

Chapter Thirteen

Heart Line II-
the Courageous Heart...

Last chapter, we looked at the short heart line. To review, your benchmark for length is an invisible line dropping down from the gap between index and middle fingers. A short heart line (starting from the pinkie side of the palm) doesn't reach this line. An average heart line does. A long heart line passes beyond it towards the thumb side of the palm.

A long heart line is relatively rare. The person with this heart line is emotionally courageous. She's totally open, trusting the Universe and people to be positive, until they individually prove themselves otherwise. (This doesn't mean she's gullible, though she may be that too. It means she has faith and trust in the innate goodness of people and things).

This can be very powerful. Since, on both a psychological and a metaphysical basis, we tend to shape our world by what we believe about it and draw to ourselves more of whatsoever we focus on, the belief that this is a good world can go a really long way towards making it so.

The long heart line can be a true challenge though. Even if your life is good, we all have times when life isn't so rosy and we have to face the tough stuff. It's easy to keep faith that all is proceeding as it should when things go well- not so easy when you stub your toe, lose your best friend, get a ticket, and you seem to be going to hell in a hand basket.....

So, having a long heart line takes great courage. The courage to say "It's raining, but I have faith that the sun will shine again, and that this world has more sunshine than showers..."

This is another time when you might want to check both palms. A long heart line in the non-dominant hand and a short one in the dominant is a trusting soul that has had her spirit crushed. It's good here to say what you can to remind her of how beautiful and courageous she has the capacity to be, and that all pain heals if you let it...

A short line in the non-dominant hand and a long one in the dominant is a wallflower who's moving out of her comfort zone.

In life, most of us wear different masks for different functions or roles we play. Not the person with the long heart line! With her, what you see is what you get. She is who she is, regardless of folks around them. Not tactless, but totally, beautifully, fully herself.

In relationships, these folks throw themselves in 110%. They're not afraid to be open and vulnerable; and get up close and personal. If their relationship fails, it's never because they didn't do everything they could. (One frequent stumbling block can be a partner with a short heart line and lots of history that leaves him afraid to be close or vulnerable. In this relationship, the long heart line may need to move s-l-o-w-l-y at her partner's speed, like coaxing a wild animal out of the wood).

These folks are beautiful, courageous and rare. If you meet one, please praise her for her many positive qualities. Encourage her to continue to be herself, rather than hide herself by conforming to others' fears.

Heart lines are usually long or short. Sometimes you will find one that stops right on the benchmark. As you might guess, that's someone who's balanced right in the middle, neither predominantly introverted nor extraverted. This is fairly rare (though not as rare as long heart lines).

This may say something interesting about the culture we live in....

Chapter Fourteen
Heart Line III
-Feelings....

Yet more heart line. ("Ya gotta have heart....")

Let's try some of those markings again.

The most common markings I see on the heart line are chains or a whole cluster of tiny branches I call "feathering", because the line ends up looking like a feather. These tend to appear in the hand of someone who has a lot of stress in their life.

Now, this has less to do with how good or bad their life is, and more to do with how they're handling it. Some people are calm and cool even if there's a hurricane blowing through and some have a meltdown if their nail polish chips. The marks indicate how well (or not) they're dealing with things.

This is stress, a less crucial and difficult area than the depression we talked about on the head line, but it does have the potential to have long-term effects on health and quality of life so it needs a bit of finesse...

Because these folks are already overwhelmed and stressed, it's important to relax them. I use exaggeration and jokes. I put on a slightly exaggerated "Hollywood fortuneteller" voice and tell them "I see a lot of stress in their life, a lot of d-r-a-m-a! You worry too much! Now if you want to worry, you can (everybody needs a hobby) but a lot of time you give all your time and energy to something that next week will be nothing to you..."

By now, they're laughing and admitting that they're constantly stressed out. This puts them in a better space to talk or think about doing things that help their good hearts calm down a bit; and focusing less on worry and more on what's juicy in their lives. I tell them that the "juice" that's used up in worry is really meant to fuel our passions, and that if they can worry less, they'll have more energy for love and creativity and everything that's "juicy" in life for them.

And, as a side effect, they'll be healthier too.

If they've got a cross on their heart line, something is keeping them from feeling or expressing their feelings. This can be an external influence or something internal (maybe a belief).

If they've got a triangle, they have special emotional gifts.

If they have a break, they may actually have a broken heart.

I met a glorious woman at a Renaissance faire one time; fashionably dressed and the center of attention in her group of followers, extravagant and very merry. I looked in her palm, saw a broken heart line, and blurted out "You poor thing, your heart is broken!"

(Whoops! I'm usually more tactful, but in this case, the information was startlingly in contrast to the impression she gave. It turned out that that blunt response was really what she needed.)

In an instant, the mask fell away and she was weeping at my table about a love affair that had ended, but that she couldn't let go of. This was something you couldn't have guessed by looking at her, and that she hadn't told a soul until now, although she desperately needed to talk about it.

That reading took a little longer than the usual. It's my way that, if someone comes to me in pain, the reading takes as long as it takes, and, if I lose money by it, so be it.

While I'm mentioning that, it is worth noting that, while many readings are "for entertainment purposes only", and some are more serious but still reasonably pleasant, you will sometimes get one where the person is having a crisis or preparing for one.

It's good to give some thought to "what would I do if someone starting crying during a reading?" (They sometimes do, you know.) Or "if someone came to me with a really serious issue (like "is my husband cheating on me?")"....

The best answer I've got is "you would do the best that you could". The specifics are up to you.

This sort of thing does happen. (I'm glad to say that a lot of the more severe ones only started to crop up after I had more experience, and was more able to handle them.) I have a few things that I do to help with this.

I have a piece of rose quartz as part of my table decorations because it creates a space of emotional safety and facilitates healing when the energy needs run that way. I've been known to have my client hold it if they're really in distress.

It's a great thing to have tissues available for use if needed.

I am a Reiki Master and have been known to run Reiki while reading (with the client's consent) for physical, mental, emotional or spiritual healing.

I pray that I may read wisely and well, according to each client's needs.

And I chose my words carefully, to empower people and to give them their control back as much as possible.

And sometimes, my clients just need a good cry and someone who will listen to them. And that's part of the job, too.

A heart line that turns upwards tends to indicate an optimistic nature. If it shoots straight upwards (frequently seen between index and middle finger) and has a lot of feathers or branches at the end, this person may be a bit of a diva or drama queen ("...see the pretty fireworks on the end of the line?..") and have a fiery nature. (Lock up the breakables and use tact...)

When looking at this portion of the palm, it's also good to look at the balance of head and heart. Which line is longer? Which line is darker? Which line naturally catches your eye more when you look at this portion of the hand?

If the head line is more prominent, this person runs their life more by thinking. "I understand" is one of their keynotes and "what?", "why?", and "how?" are going to be frequent flyers in their conversations. Things will not be let in the door unless they "make sense".

If the heart line is more prominent, this person flies by feelings and gut reactions. "That feels right" is their touchstone. They'll be concerned with motivations, with understanding why people take actions and if experiences feel comfortable or not. Things are not let in the door unless they "feel right".

You will sometimes see someone where both lines are perfectly balanced. These folks are equally comfortable in either style.

Now, neither style is superior to the other. There are many kinds of circumstances in life. Some are better suited to the head line style and some to the heart line. We all also have the ability to work out of the method which is not our automatic approach (for feelers to use pure logic, and thinkers to trust their guts) but we tend to be best at the style that we use most.

It's a good idea, though, to be aware of your primary style so that you know when you'll be playing to your strengths and when it might be better to have someone with a different approach take the lead.

You'll often find that you end up interacting (in love, in work, on committees) with someone with that opposite approach. You'll get the best results if you don't try to make them see things your way, but rather use the words and images, as well as the approaches, that translate into their language (for it is like another language). For example, asking a head line person "what doesn't make sense to you?" or a heart line person "what would it take to reach a result that you'd feel good about?"

Now, what happens when the head and heart lines overlap?.....

Chapter Fifteen

The Simian Line-
Not Monkeying Around.....

In a majority of palms, there are two major lines crossing the palm horizontally. The lower one (closer to the thumb) is the head line. The higher one (closer to the fingers) is the heart line.

Once in a very long while, instead of two lines, you'll see a single line; one that looks like the head and heart lines are occupying the same exact space.

This is called a simian line. In theory, it has this name because that's the way the hands of monkeys and apes are marked. (I cannot speak with any personal authority on this myself, as I have neither personally looked at the hand of anyone in the simian family, nor looked at photos of same. This is just what I've heard....)

According to tradition, the simian line appeared in the hands of maniacs and murderers and the criminally insane; people who were extremely violent or crazy or both (and not in a good way). In short, people who one would think twice about sitting holding hands with (or, for that matter, being in the same county with).

My experience of people with simian lines is somewhat different, and has colored my interpretation of what the line means. (My experience in this area has been limited, but very informative.)

I find that folks with simian lines are not violent or crazy per se, although they do have the capacity to be so. The key characteristics of people with these lines seems to be that they're highly impulsive and will often act without thinking about what that action will mean for them in the long run. They feel things very deeply and react abruptly.

Often, they can have hot tempers.

Most of us chose to act in keeping with what society finds appropriate. Most of us also have "safety catches" in our brains that keep us from acting without thinking. In the case of folks with simian lines, it is as if those safety catches and social norms either do not exist, or else are so weak that they have no control over impulsivity.

To give a couple of examples of people I've met with simian lines, one was a man who'd been a soldier severely brain injured in war who now had a plate in his head. Since his injury, his impulse control had gone severely down and he frequently did things without thinking that he regretted later on (stated by the man and confirmed by his loving but much put upon girlfriend. They both confirmed she did a lot of damage control on messes that he created). This man had a simian line in his dominant hand but not his non-dominant.

Another man I met had a hot temper and felt like people were mostly against him. On occasion, he was known to put a hole in the wall with his fist, when he felt that someone was making fun of him. He had simian lines in both hands.

So what do you, the reader, do if you see a simian line? Well, first and foremost, you're going to choose your words extra carefully and kindly. (In my closet, I have a button saying "Use tact, you fathead!" for just such an occasion.) You chose your words carefully so your client can hear and benefit from what you're saying and so you don't say something that causes a knee-jerk reaction that you'll both regret later on.

Then, you talk to this person about looking before you leap, about needing to think before you act, and, if they're receptive, to finding what kind of things work for them if they start to get a little hot under the collar. I'll gauge my client and, if I feel it'll work for him, I'll make a little joke about him being a rascal and getting himself into difficulties by acting before he thinks about it. All the while, I'll be watching his body language and, if he starts to tense up, I know that I'm going down the wrong road for him and need to back up and take a different route.

So you do the best you can to do right by your client and empower him, rather than setting him off.

(By the by, I do not know if this characteristic is gender linked. I do know that the few ones I've seen have all been male.)

Figure 3 – Miscellaneous Marks

A – Thumb Chain
B - Marriage Lines
C – Bracelets

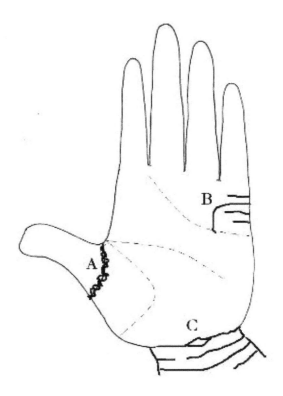

Figure 3 – Miscellaneous Marks

Chapter Sixteen

Thumb-Thing You Should Know

Now we're going on to a couple of things to look at concerning your thumb. Please consult Figure 3, "Miscellaneous Marks".

First, we're going to look at something called a "thumb chain". (See item "A" on your handout to locate this.) At the base of your thumb, most people have some kind of line circling the entire base.

On many people (or at least many of the people that I see), this line will be a chain for most or all of the line. (Remember chains from your marks handout?). What does that mean? Well, a thumb chain appears in the hand of someone who's naturally stubborn......

Now, this can be a good thing and/or a bad thing.

On the plus side, this person has the persistence to finish what they start (assuming it's worth finishing. Sometimes you start something and then discover that it isn't what you thought it would be and is therefore not worth putting in more time and energy on it.)

This person also has the strength to hang in there when times get tough and see things through.

These are powerful skills.

On the flip side, sometimes it's time to let go. Folks with this chain have no clue whatsoever about how to let go. (As someone born under the astrological sign of Cancer with thumb chains on both hands, I'm certainly not looking down on this mind set - just calling it like it is.)

This can be a major disadvantage....

Now, how do you approach this information with the querant with the thumb chain? My experience is that, if you just say "You're stubborn!" these folks tend to snap back "No, I'm not!" and things go downhill from there.

So, being me, I start with a joke...

I point it out and say (with delight), "Oh, a thumb chain! I see a lot of these! These tend to belong to people who are a teeny, weeny bit stubborn..."

At this point, the querant (and any buddies he's got...) invariably crack up and says he's VERY stubborn. I grin and tell him "That's right. I was just trying to be polite!..." and we go on from here. The querant's now relaxed, in a good mood and able to actually hear and benefit from what I've got to tell him. (This works for me because I'm short and cute. You may need to vary your approach based on who you are...)

What do I tell him then? I start with the two strengths I noted above, which are useful and positive aspects to this characteristic. I then talk about the actual stubbornness.

I quote W.C. Fields, who said "If at first you don't succeed, try, try again. Then give up! There's no use being a damned fool about it!" (I tell him Fields was speaking to folks like he and I). If he needs a little more loosening up, I show him <u>my</u> thumb chain to show him that we're in this together.

I acknowledge that letting go of something can be very difficult. I tell him he might want to form a partnership with someone he respects and trusts who'll every now and then tell him kindly but firmly that "it's time to let it go!"

Just for fun, an interesting side-note on the thumb chain. Something else useful ......

How do you get a person with a thumb chain to co-operate with you? After all, they're stubborn so they make terrible opponents as they will hang in there when lesser mortals fall away.

You won't be able to intimidate them. Or shame them. Or coerce, or seduce, or pressure them.

The best way to get a person with a thumb chain as your ally is to show them how doing what **you** want will benefit them and help them get what they want. (You need to know what makes them tick for this to work).

Then they'll be as stubborn on your behalf as they might otherwise be against you....

Bonus information- If you're meeting someone you need to work co-operatively with, when you shake their hand, tilt it slightly outwards and take a peek. Most times, you should be able to see if they have a thumb chain or not. (This'll only work if they're right handed). This gives you useful insight to help you form a relationship that'll work for you both.

Sometimes, you'll find a person that has only a partial chain (chained for half and regular line for the rest).These folks are stubborn in certain areas but not in others.

Folks whose thumb line is not chained aren't stubborn.

Folks whose thumb line is broken or only partial tend to lack focus. They start things but don't finish them (and not because the activity proves to not be worth finishing). They tend to have a drawer, or a box, or even a closet full of half-finished projects they're going to finish "someday".

They need to be reminded that the things they create deserve to see the light of day and that they need to work on seeing things through to completion. Give them the positive strokes they need to stick with it.

<u>Hand Notes</u>

Some other names for palmistry are dactylomancy, chirosophy, chiromancy, and cheiromancy.

Chapter Seventeen

Thumb-Thing Else You Should Know

Last time, we talked about the thumb chain and stubbornness. This time, let's talk about another characteristic of the thumb - flexibility....

First and foremost, how do we evaluate thumb flexibility? For starters, I'd recommend that, if possible, you go and get someone else to try this out on. You can try it on yourself but it's much easier on someone else, especially when you're starting out.

Before you start, tell the querant you're going to move his thumb and ask if he has any medical problems (ex: arthritis, injury, etc,) that might affect doing that.

Always move the thumb gently. If there's a medical problem, go extra gently and watch your client for any facial grimaces, wincing, etc., that indicate you're causing pain or pushing too far. The idea is to check for flexibility and you need to be sure to move within your client's tolerance.

Cradle the person's dominant hand in one of yours. (This usually works out to be your dominant hand, but not necessarily...) Turn his hand palm up.

With your thumb, index and middle fingers of your other hand (the non-cradling one), grasp the tip of his thumb. Move it gently until it is positioned over the edge of his palm, parallel with his index finger (as if it were a stick shift in "neutral", for those of you who remember manual transmissions.)

Gently, bend the thumb backwards (i.e. - the opposite way to which the thumb usually goes). Some thumbs are very flexible and will waggle all over the place. Some are so stiff you can hardly move them. Most fall on the gradient somewhere in between.

To get good information for the client, you'll need to classify him mentally as "stiff" or "flexible", although this is actually a range of how stiff or flexible one is. To get a good feel for this, especially when you're starting out, it's good to try this out on as many people as possible, to get a good feel for it.

The flexibility of a thumb (or lack of it) indicates how well that person handles change....

The person with a stiff thumb (and that's the majority of people) doesn't handle change well. The more stiff the thumb, the less he likes it.

On the plus side, this person doesn't waste his time on fads. On the other hand, he's so naturally cautious that, when something comes along that's meant for him, by the time he's ready to try it, it's often gone....

I usually tell folks like this that "change is not your good buddy". I acknowledge the plus side but cue them in on how they can lose out. I then ask them if they want to know the secret of how to get around this.....

Yes, there is a secret. People like this may not like change but they can learn a way to chose to reach out to the changes that are right for them.

I tell these folks that we all have a public self and a true self. Life can tend to pull us away from our true selves and our true missions by distracting us with all of the other stuff (and there is an awful lot of that "other stuff"...).

If you find and do the things that keeps you in touch with your true self and your true mission (which may or may not have anything to do with your job), when something new comes along that's meant for you, it'll sing in your soul. You'll think "oh, that's not a stranger-it's just an old friend I haven't met yet!" Then you'll take what's meant for you, let go of the rest, and have the best of all possible worlds....

What are the things to get you in touch with your true self and your true mission? It's very different for every person. For some, it's meditation or prayer. For others, reading inspirational or self-help books. For some, it's deep reflection, or time in nature, or analyzing where one's time and energy go, or setting a personal mission statement.

The path to enlightenment is different for each of us. I'll give the folks with the stiff thumb some of these examples but tell them that the important thing is to find what works for them and then be sure they do it on a regular basis.

Just to stay in touch with their dreams. Then the rest will follow....

<u>Hand Notes</u>

Historically, written records of palmistry go back as far as 2000 B.C. in India.

Chapter Eighteen

Thumb-Thing Additional

The last chapter looked at a client's thumb flexibility and how it indicates their tolerance for novelty and change. We covered how to check a thumb's flexibility, what a stiff thumb indicates and things to tell someone who has one.

Now let's look at the opposite end of the spectrum....

Sometimes you'll run into a person whose thumb bends backwards easily and fluidly. There's little resistance as you waggle his thumb around and no tension.

The person with the flexible thumb likes change. He enjoys trying new things just for novelty's sake. (One thing I tell folks like this is "If it's new, it's for you!". They immediately beam brightly and chortle at me.)

Now, this is a relatively unusual trait. Most of us are hardwired with varying degrees of resistance to change. My theory is that this goes back to the dawn of time when something new and unfamiliar might eat you or otherwise harm you before you figured it out, whereas you were more likely to survive things you knew how to safely deal with. Resistance to change could therefore become a survival trait....

That's one theory why there are so many people with stiff thumbs walking around out there.

In practice, however, because change is inevitable and most people can't handle change, our flexible thumb folks have an automatic advantage over most of the people around them (since change is no longer as potentially lethal as it used to be, even though most of us are still acting like it is.)

Tell your client this. Tell him his willingness to try new things gives him that advantage over most folks. Pat him on the back for this.

As I find myself frequently saying during readings, everything has a good side and a not so good side. The positive side of the flexible thumb is his ability to handle change well, and even enjoy it.

The disadvantage is that the person with a flexible thumb likes to please people. He likes to please them so much, he'll over-promise. He'll promise folks the moon and the stars on a silver platter. Then, if he can only deliver the moon, as opposed to being impressed with that, they start saying "What about those stars? You said there would be stars!..." and they get angry with him.

This person needs to learn that, if he promises less and delivers more, he'll actually make people happier.

A person with a flexible thumb combined with an over-developed mound of Saturn needs to watch out for a tendency to enable his partner in a codependent relationship. (Saturn deals with responsibility and we'll be going over it considerably further along in this book.)

One other thing to note on these aspects of the thumb. For some reason, these two issues (stubbornness and the ability, or lack thereof, to deal with change) are very compelling pieces of information. People who don't believe in psychic phenomena will often become believers because of what the thumb has to say.

If you do enough readings, there are two very special kinds of people you will eventually run into.

One kind are debunkers. These are people who have decided that there is no such thing as psychic phenomenon and "don't confuse them with the facts". No matter what you say or do, even if you produce the shade of Harry Houdini playing the trumpet backed by a full angelic choir, they will tune out anything that doesn't suit their beliefs. They will find some way to twist what you've said, ignore anything that doesn't suit their own limited world view or actually create things you never said or did in order to maintain their "safe" belief of how the world is or shore up their crippled self-esteem by putting you down.

A debunker will probably not sit in your chair to begin with. (They'd rather hover in front of your table and make snide comments). If they do sit down, they're there to find fault and you'll know them pretty quickly by what they say and how they say it.

Don't bother trying to convince a debunker. (He's putting all his energy into blocking out any proof.) It is possible to sometimes take them off-guard and open their minds a crack, but that's random chance so don't be too attached to it. (As W.C. Fields used to say "Never try to teach a pig to sing. It only wastes your time and annoys the pig.") Don't let them get you angry or in escalating arguments. It won't go anywhere and you'll only make yourself look bad.

Just try to have a gentle, polite or cute way of turning their anger aside prepared

Some examples:

- for the low-grade teenaged smart alec who keeps shouting "Tell me what I'm thinking!" I grin and say "You're thinking I can't do it!....";
- for the more aggressive nasty man, I'll ask him innocently and LOUDLY why, if he thinks this isn't real, why he wants to hang around it so much...)
What's right depends on the case.

And feel some compassion for them. They come from a buttoned-down world and they really don't feel good about themselves. That's why they're angry at you. They see you as more free than they can ever be.

The other kind of special person are the skeptics (Love those skeptics!.....) These are people who either aren't sure whether there's true psychic phenomenon or not, or don't believe in it but have open enough minds to listen to and evaluate new information and adjust their beliefs based on their experiences.

I've heard quite a number of psychics say they can't be bothered with reading for skeptics (or teenagers, or little children, or anyone else who will not fall down and kiss their shoes evidently. Only true believers need apply.).

I've never understood that. I love reading for skeptics. Usually they're reasonably polite and open, but you need to bring your "A" game to convince them. This really makes me stretch my skills to give them a reading that will work for them (which makes me a better reader the more that I do it...).

And, oh, that wonderful moment when a skeptic has a "cosmic a-ha!" and realizes that, while the sign may say ""for entertainment purposes only", that this is the real deal. The look that flashes across their faces when they see that the universe is far bigger and brighter and more magical than they had realized until that moment....

I just love it! I love reading for skeptics!

So, why do I mention this here? For this reason - in my experience, the two "thumb-things" we've covered in the last 3 chapters are ten times (twenty times? a hundred times?) more likely than any other facet to transform a skeptic to a believer in one fell swoop!

Why?

Don't know. Just know it's so.

You may find other individual characteristics may be compelling for folks on a case by case basis, but time after time, it's the thumb that changes everything.

Chapter Nineteen

Marriage Lines-
The People who Rock Our World

One of the most requested areas in readings is, of course, romance. Part of this information lies on the heart line, which tells us about your emotional skills and gives us information on how ready you are for romance and for how you'll function within it, amongst other things.

Another question in this topic is "when will I find romance?" To quote a cliché, the traditional "tall, dark stranger coming into your life." Marriage lines tell us when such opportunities are likely...

Contrary to their name, marriage lines do not necessarily mean marriages. They can mean marriages, yes. Or Significant Romances without benefit of Ring or Ceremony. Or really good friends (the kind that you'd die for). Or teachers or mentors who change your life.

I think of marriage lines as standing for the People Who Rock Our World.

It's also worthy of note that marriage lines do not have to be exclusively for humans. If you fell down the well when you were 5 and almost died but Lassie pulled you out, you might actually have a marriage line for Lassie....

Let's start with how to find when these important people are coming into someone's life.

First, you have to know the life expectancy. Remember, back in chapter 7, we discussed how to find someone's life expectancy and how to locate when different things were going to occur in their life by looking at the life line? I mentioned at that time that, even if the person didn't want to know his life expectancy, you needed to know this in order to apply that amount of time to other landmarks with time lines later on in the palm. Well, here's the first one.

That was awhile back (12 chapters, to be exact). You may need to go back and check the life expectancy again. You may even need to review chapter 7 again on how to read a time line.

Go ahead - I'll wait.....

Ready? Do you know the life expectancy of the palm you're looking at (whether it's someone else's or your own)? Now we're going to take that amount of time and apply it to another area.

Technically, we're not going to be reading the palm here but rather the side of the hand. Take the dominant hand and hold it gently. Grasp the tip of the pinkie with the thumb and forefingers of your other hand and pull it out to the side, away from the ring finger, as far as it will go without forcing it. (Gently! If we're not gentle, we can pull the finger out of the socket and that's no fun for anyone...).

At this point, little horizontal lines will pop out on the side of the hand under the base of the pinkie. These are the marriage lines. For a visual reference, please look at Figure 3, "Miscellaneous Marks". The marriage lines are landmark "B".

Now it's time to use that life expectancy. We're going to project that time span on the side of the hand, covering the space from the line circling the base of the pinkie (which stands for the beginning of life) to the point where the heart line runs around the side of the hand (which indicates the end of life).

For instance, if you had someone whose life line indicates that she will live for 80 years, that tiny space will cover 80 years of meeting the most seriously significant people in her life.

And, if there's a line 1/4 of the way down, a significant person will show up at 20. And, if halfway down, at 40. And so forth...

Sound familiar? You've done this before, just in a different (and larger) space.

Your mileage may vary. Please adjust to allow for the original life expectancy in that space on the side of your hand (for example, with a ninety year life expectancy, ½ way down would be 45 and 1/3 way down would be 30, and so forth).

Both traditional thought and personal experience tell us that the longer and deeper a marriage line is, the more significant the relationship will be. The lighter or shorter it is, the less. (This will still be a significant relationship since only significant relationships appear at all in this way).

I've also heard the theory (although I cannot speak to its accuracy) that a marriage line that turns down and runs into the heart line indicates a divorce. I don't know if that's so, but I do know that marriage lines change and come and go more frequently than some other lines.

If a person has had a marriage and a divorce but is still carrying energy from that relationship with her, the line continues to appear in her hand. If, on the other hand, the marriage is ended and the person has cleared its energy out of her head and heart, the line will vanish.

I actually know about the more transitory nature of marriage lines from personal experience. I originally had quite a number of light marriage lines. This changed radically when I fell in love with the man I later married. The little "fooling around" lines vanished and I was left with one deep, clear marriage line right around the time we became serious. (We were friends first, but the line appeared once I was smitten. But that's another story....)

So how do you read for romance? Sometimes I'll incorporate it in the structure of a standard reading. (More on structure later on). Sometimes I'll ask if the querant has any particular concerns.

If "**Love**" comes up, (that and "**Money**" tie for most frequent), I'll ask how old the querant is now. I'll look at the marriage lines to see when significant people are current due to show up compared to the present.

I'll also sneak a peek at the heart line (if the tall, dark stranger is coming soon) to see if the querant is ready to receive him. If her heart line is short, she's shy or cautious and may have trouble holding up her end of a relationship. If her heart has been harmed (longer in non-dominant than dominant- remember?), this person has some healing or emotional housekeeping to do before she's ready to be in a serious full relationship.

I'll always start by telling the querant of all the different types of people a marriage line can indicate, and that the fact that the side of her hand is busy doesn't necessarily mean she's going to marry many times.

Sometimes she listens. Often she doesn't ("Look, Shirley, the psychic says I'm going to get married seven times!!!").

Sigh. But at least I tried......

I'll show her the marriage lines and how to monitor them herself (Clients love to know how to do this and it's a simple task, not beyond a beginner. It can help her monitor whether she's doing the kind of things with her life to head towards her special someone. Or someones...)

(It's also fun at parties…)

I give her an overview of when to expect significant people to show up throughout life and focus on the quality of the relationship closest to her present age (or the best one, if the present one's not so good.)

If there's not a relationship currently on the radar in the now or near-now, I remind her about free will and tell her that, if she continues to do things the way she has been doing them, she's not currently headed towards romance. If she wants romance, she's going to have to change how she's doing things.

I also may talk about openness and whether she might need to do a little work to be prepared to be a better romantic partner. Shy or hurting people often need to do some emotional housecleaning before they're prepared to get truly close to someone and trust them. Closeness and trust can make or break a relationship.

And I always try to put a positive spin on what's on the hand.

Because there always is a positive way to look at it.

Chapter Twenty

Children Lines-
And Baby Makes Three!

In the last chapter, we looked at marriage lines which (as you recall) indicate significant relationships in the querant's life. This chapter, we'll be looking at the children lines.

Just as "marriage lines" do not always stand for marriages, but rather for significant relationships; so also "children lines" do not exclusively mean children. They stand for children or other creative offshoots from the relationship indicated by the marriage line. (Remember-some of the relationships indicated by marriage lines are significant but platonic, with no offspring involved.)

"Children lines" can stand for children.

If they are children, they can be children of the body (ones you carried through pregnancy yourself), children by law (by adoption or by marrying someone with their own children that you end up parenting yourself), or children of the spirit (ones you have no legal ties to, but end up parenting for all practical purposes).

"Children lines" can also stand for a relationship's creative offshoots that are not people, little or otherwise. For example, if one marriage line stood for a mentor that you collaborated with to write a book, if the book and the mentor were significant enough to you, you'd have a marriage line for the mentor and a child line for the book.

How does one find the children lines? Well, we start with the marriage lines....

Looking on the dominant hand, follow a marriage line around to the end that is on the palm. At this point, you stop and look for forks or branches. Each branch or fork stands for a child or other creative offshoot from the relationship.

Remember back in chapter 5, where I said that forks or tassels are usually negative, but that there are a few places where they are neutral or good? Well this is one of the good ones (unless, of course, you don't want children....).

No forks? This indicates one or no children (because you can't have a fork with only one branch. Kinda Zen, that.)

When you were looking at marriage lines, the closer a line was to the top/pinkie edge of the palm, the earlier in life that relationship would take place. Children lines are similar to this. The branch that is highest on the palm is the first child; the next one down, the second; and so forth.

It does not always happen, but children lines can also appear for a child that has been miscarried.

Children lines (like other lines) can be light or dark.

Tradition holds that dark lines are boys and light lines girls.

I tend to think that the dark lines are boys or really dynamic girls; and the light lines are girls or really gentle boys. To me, it seems to deal more with energy (yin or yang) than plumbing.

Sometimes, you'll get someone who wants, during their palm reading, to know more about their children than whether they will have any and whether they will be boys or girls. They'll want to know about their children's health, or happiness, or career options.

Palm reading is primarily about the person being read and other folks primarily come into it in regards to how they interact with the querant.

Don't despair, though. If this kind of situation comes up, you can default to the techniques I'll be discussing near the end of this book for answering more specific questions or ones with limited feedback in the palm itself. (We'll be discussing using a pendulum and using your own intuition to get such additional information.) These methods work well for letting Mom know if Suzy will find a good career, or Joe is going to straighten out his life without help from her.

Chapter Twenty One

Bracelets-
The Perfect Rapid Reading

In the past two chapters, we've been off of the palm proper and have been reading the marriage and children lines. These hang out on the side of the hand.

Continuing in that vein, we're next going to look at the lines called "bracelets" which appear, appropriately enough, on your inner wrist. For a visual reference, please look at Figure 3, "Miscellaneous Marks". The bracelets are landmark "C".

Bracelets are the lines circling or partially circling your wrist below the base of your palm. They are read in order from top to bottom (or closer to palm to farther away, if you are dangling upside down from the top of a tower, for instance...).

In order:

The first one is health.

The second one is wealth.

The third one (and any thereafter) is happiness.

Any bracelets after the first three are considered additional happiness bracelets. (How nice! If I was offered a shot of something extra, happiness would be my first choice!...)

The ideal bracelet goes all the way across the inner wrist, is deep and well-defined, and has positive marking and no negative markings upon it.

Many times, that's not what you'll see.

If a bracelet only goes part way across the wrist or is broken, there are problems in that area. For instance, I only have half a health bracelet and have serious health issues, including asthma and chronic fatigue syndrome.

If a bracelet is light, there's a lack of that characteristic.

If it contains an island, there's some kind of negative

limitations in that area. For instance, on the wealth bracelet, the depth of the line would indicate how much money you have, and an island would indicate a situation where there was money you couldn't put your hands on (such as a trust).

If a bracelet has chaining, there's conflict surrounding issues in that area.

If a bracelet has a triangle, a special gift or windfall in that area.

A bracelet with forks or feathers indicates a lot of waste or drama in that area. (Easy come - easy go.)

Sometimes, you'll see a happiness bracelet that's well-defined but very light. This stands for someone who's got wonderful opportunities for happiness, but is so busy that he doesn't actually use them. Sometimes you'll even see two or more happiness bracelets that are very light. These persons need to stop what they're doing and smell the roses now!

Having already worked a bit with the marks from handout 1, I'm sure that you're getting the feel for how they apply here.

Bracelets are not, by themselves, a fully in-depth reading, but they do make a wonderful overview for occasions when you need to either give a quick reading or a lot of readings in a relatively short period of time. They cover three of the major topics folks want to know about in a simple, straightforward manner.

Bracelets are also wonderful to start out with if you're teaching a bit of palmistry to beginners (whether beginners in palmistry or in doing readings in general). Even if you don't have enough time to teach your students all about the marks you've started with, they can still benefit from a simple version of "Health-Wealth-Happiness" that looks at length and definition of the bracelets. This is a useful technique that is also fun at parties.

Chapter Twenty-Two
The Simple Reading

With the information that you've learned in the last twenty-one chapters, you now have enough knowledge under your belt to do a simple or basic palm reading, one similar to the one I was doing when I was in college (over 40 years ago, back when dinosaurs walked the Earth...). It does not cover everything but does touch on a good share of the basics. From my experience, it's very satisfying to most people (especially if the reading you're giving is a free one for family or friends, just for fun).

In this lesson, I'm going to go over a simple format for doing this, pulling together the various elements in an order that'll be coherent and make sense, both for your client and for you. This format is only a suggestion and, if you prefer or are guided to put things in a different order, please do so. (Free Will rules!)

First and foremost, it's important to tell your querant about Free Will - how they have the power to change their futures and how their palms will change as they do so. This may seem rather pedantic, like something for students but not clients, but, without this information, a palm reading can become a self-fulfilling prophesy that can push a client into bad experiences.

That's not what a reading is meant to be.

A good reading should give your client the information they need to empower them to make better choices to have a better life. If they don't know about Free Will, don't know that they can change their lives by changing their choices, and that palms change to reflect this, your reading will not be the empowering experience it was meant to be. (99% of people don't know this and are surprised when you tell them.)

So, tell them about Free Will. Please. As your teacher, I charge you with doing this so that you are reading ethically.

They'll ask you which palm you read. Ask about their hand
dominance (which hand they eat with). Read both palms, emphasizing
the dominant as we previously discussed. If you like, you can explain why you're prioritizing that hand. A bit of education is a good thing and gives you a chance to get organized.

If their palm isn't relaxed, get it into that relaxed, cupped position.

Now is the time to look things over and get oriented before you start telling them things. You'll be quiet for a moment or two, which may feel like eternity....

Don't worry - it isn't. Your client will wait. If it makes you or her more comfortable, you can say "Just a minute while I get my bearings here..." or something similar.

Look at the life line. Start by looking at life expectancy for your reference point. Ask if she wants to know how long she's going to live. (This is one of the two things in a palm that scare folks the most).

If she wants to know, tell her. If she doesn't, don't. (You can make a general statement about a good long life-if it's true, of course.) In either case, please re-emphasize free will here, and how she can change her life expectancy.

Ask her how old she is; if she doesn't mind telling you. (Most won't, although some may want to whisper.) Look at the section of life line that she's currently living. Are there any markings? Cue her in on what's happening now or what she should watch out for soon. If there are no markings, talk about life being relatively straight forwards.

You can talk to her about chi or vital force. Does she have a double or triple life line? Is it lighter one place and darker another? Cue her in on when she'll be slowing down and when she'll be up and boogieing.

If you see changeling markings, talk to her about being her own person, whether or not her family gets it. (This one's crucial. There are a lot of wounded changelings out there drifting around feeling like there's something wrong with them, just because they're different from their families!)

Look at the head line. Talk to her about brains - what she has and how much she's using them. Talk to her about creativity, and about remembering to have fun.

If you see signs of vulnerability to depression, be sensitive when you talk to her about it. Remind her to take care of herself.

Look at the heart line. Is she an open or private person? Talk to her about the pluses and minuses of the path she's walking.

Are there masses of chains, indicating stress or "d-r-a-m-a!"? Tell her that, and talk to her about learning to manage stress so she has more energy for the positive things she's passionate about.

Look at the thumb. Thumb chain? If so, talk to her about the ups and downs of stubbornness. If no, talk to her about working on focus and carrying through on things.

How flexible is that thumb? How well can your querant handle change? There's another topic to go over.

Check out the marriage and children lines. Here's another good place to re-emphasize the impact of free will.

Finally, go over the bracelets. Health, wealth and happiness - the big three.

Throughout, remember to tell the truth. (That's why readers were formerly called soothsayers - we say sooth/tell the truth) Be positive and empowering. That's how your reading can be a blessing to your querant.

Make eye contact, smile and be ready to listen. (Sometimes a reading is a place for the querant to talk to someone kind and receptive. Don't get so hung up on getting your reading out that you talk over a querant who really needs to talk to someone herself).

Pay attention to your querant's face and body language; and what she says. It's your job to tell her what's really there, but to do it in a way so that she can hear and benefit from it. Her verbal and non-verbal feedback will tell you things such as:

1) Is this person confused about what I'm saying?

2) Do I need to use simpler words?

3) Do I need to find another way to say this because the phrases I'm using aren't connecting with this person?

4) Is this person scared? Do I have to find a gentler way to give her this information?

5) Am I going too fast?

6) Does this person need to talk?

7) Is this person not interested in the section I'm talking about? Do we need to go to another area of the palm?

8) Is this person's brain full? Does she need to stop a minute and think about what I've said or ask a question?

9) Does this person need me to be more serious, in respect to what she's going through?

10) Does she need me to lighten the mood with a joke or story so she can relax and absorb the information I'm giving her?

…And other exciting questions such as these. The feedback your querant gives you will help you get in sync with her so you can give her a better, more customized reading that will better serve her need.

Chapter Twenty-Three

How to Get the Most Out of This Book
(And Optional Homework)

At this point, you've got a lot of palmistry information under your belt. Now I'm going to talk about how to get the most out of it.

If you want to get the maximum benefits from this book, there are 6 things you should be doing.

1) Read the chapters. (It's good to read them one by one, as opposed to in a great mass, as it'll give each chapter a chance to sink in before you get to the next one, but I know that not everyone's life is conducive to this. I understand - but it's still a good idea...)

2) Look at your palm after you've read a chapter to see what you can see from that chapter in your palm.

3) Look at both of your palms - they're different and you'll learn things by looking at both of them.

4) Look at the palms of other people around you. As many as you can. The more palms you look at to transfer these lessons to real experience, the faster you'll learn and the more proficient you'll be. (I understand that some people are shy about doing this publicly. If you're not or if you can get past that shyness, you'll learn so much more if you're practicing on lots of lovely people!)

5) Practice, practice, practice!

And....

6) Try the optional homework that goes with this chapter.

Optional homework is one way that I've designed to help people transform this knowledge into something meaningful and real for them on an individual basis. Some people want to learn divination and other metaphysical skills, but are too shy to share this with other people, or are in a position where they do not feel comfortable or safe being openly metaphysical. It gives you a chance to actively practice without having a study buddy, or revealing your metaphysical abilities to the world at large.

If you're not that shy or closeted, but still want to maximize your learning, the optional homework is still great to do. It gives you more practice, and practice is what will help you to both learn this knowledge and become better at using it.

That being said, whether you do it or not is up to you.

The optional homework is, like everything else in this book, optional (hence the name). That means you do it, and/or as many of the other options listed above as you can do and want to do in order to get the most out of the book.

And no more...

I want you to learn well, have fun, and become the best palmist your interest, energy, life style and other responsibilities will permit, without making yourself crazy in the process.....

Well, not unhappily crazy.

Happily crazy, I'm good with.

So chose to do what works for you....

Now for the audience participation portion of the chapter....

For those of you who've decided to do the optional homework, go to Figures 4 and 5, "Optional Homework I- Palm 1" and "Optional Homework -Palm 2".

Everybody there? Good!

Now, your mission (should you chose to accept it) is to look at the palms pictured and tell me as much as you can about these people.

Assume that these are dominant hands.

In the next chapter I'll be reviewing these palms. It's a good idea to form your opinions on these palms before you look at mine. Let's see what you get...

Figure 4 – Optional Homework I – Palm 1

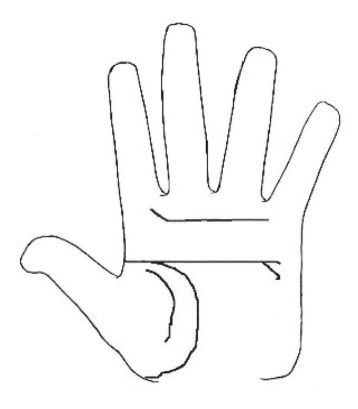

Figure 4 – Optional Homework I – Palm 1

Figure 5 – Optional Homework I – Palm 2

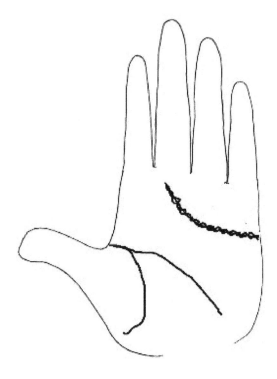

Figure 5 – Optional Homework I - Palm 2

Chapter Twenty-Four

Optional Homework -
The Basic Palm - Some Answers

The last chapter reviewed the many ways that you can learn from this book and get the most out of it.

You can read the chapters.

You can practice on yourself.

You can practice on other people (the more the better)

Amongst the options available to help you learn is the "optional homework" section that goes with the last chapter.

Now, I know that everyone has full lives, lots of commitments, and very full schedules. Despite this, I'm sure that everyone reading this has looked at the handouts and at least gotten some ideas about the owners of the palms pictured in their heads.

(You have, haven't you?...)

(By the by, the palms pictured in these handouts are totally fictitious and should not be confused with any actual people, whether living or dead...

In other words, I made them up.)

So, let's look at these palms together....

Let's try some simple questions, for structure's sake. Some answers will be following.....

Palm 1

How long will this person live?

What is his personality like?

What do his closets look like?

Can you tell me anything else?

Palm 2

How long will this person live?

What is her personality like?
Is she creative?
Can you tell me anything else about her?

Palm 1

He is a strong and very energetic man. He has amazing energy through his early 70s, then slows to normal human energy thereafter, but never becomes frail. His life expectancy is at least 100 if he doesn't use his free will too foolishly to mess up his future.

He is a logical and organized person. (His closets are therefore organized and full of labeled storage units.).

He is a linear thinker and solves problems step by step.

He has a bit of a gift for writing and probably uses an outline to structure his writing so it proceeds directly to a specific objective.

He is outgoing and open. What you see with him is what you get.

His head rules the roost. To get in his life, things need to make sense, and if you wish to persuade him of something, you need to logically show him the positive nature of it.

Palm 2

She has a life expectancy of 83-85.

She has close ties with her family.

She is very intelligent and creative. She is full of amazing and unusual ideas.

Unfortunately, she's got problems emotionally. She's got mountains of stress (which can be due to what happens to her or how she chooses to view it).

She's also depressed and withdrawn.

She uses logic to keep her from crashing and burning.

Sadly, this is currently not enough. She needs a better strategy that'll make sense to her.

I'd check her non-dominant hand. If it's more cheerful than this one, the implication would be that prolonged stress is dragging her into depression, at which point she needs to do something to change course. If both hands are similar, she's naturally private and more easily overwhelmed.

She needs some TLC and careful guidance to get her back on an uphill path where she can thrive as opposed to just survive.

The information in the readings of the optional homework palms above comes out of the information you've gotten in the previous 23 chapters applied to the pictures on the optional homework sheet. This includes life expectancy, mood and affect, thinking style, social skills and all of the other goodies. (Palm 1's closet is an extrapolation based on his very logical head line). I'm sure that you're looking back at the handout as you read these answers and seeing how the different landmarks yield each piece of information.

Now that you've got the elements and the structure of the basic reading and have had the opportunity to practice combining those pieces, we can move on to more advanced topics.

Figure 6- Fate Line, Fame Line, Health Line

A – Fate Line
B – Fame Line
C – Health Line

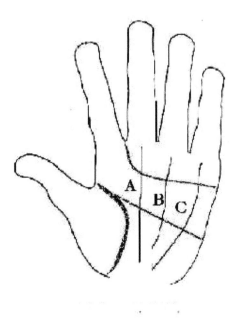

Figure 6 – Fate Line, Fame Line, Health Line

Chapter Twenty-Five

Fate Line I -
The Cornucopia of the Palm

We've gone over the basics of ethical soothsaying and the effects of Free Will in a reading. We've talked about empowering your client, and how the right words can make a major difference in how well your querant can hear and benefit from the information you've seen for them. We've explored the markings found throughout the landmarks of the palm. We've reviewed the three primary lines, the influence of the thumb, marriage lines, and bracelets. We've looked at how they all fit together in a substantial basic reading.

In short, we've gotten you well grounded and able to do the basic reading for family, friends and clients.

Whew! Take a deep breath...

Because now it's time to expand the scope of our readings by adding additional landmarks.

This chapter begins examining the fate line. This line covers luck and money, and is where most material goodies hang out.

Because most people obtain money by earning it, your job tends to primarily be located here. (There are other indicators of profession, professional interests, and professional skills scattered about the palm, but this line is the primary indicator, especially of what "is" as opposed to what we might want.)

It's worthy of note that, if you get your income through your partner or parent working, this line would indicate the influence of his or her work and income, in the context that it influences you and you influence it. (If your partner makes a lot of money but only gives you a little, what you receive will be what's on your palm). If you live off inherited money, this line would be about that.

This is where you show them the money....

To locate the fate line, please consult Figure 6, "Fate, Fame and Health Lines". The fate line is a vertical line (labeled "A" on the illustration) that starts at the bottom of the palm and runs upwards, ending somewhere under the middle finger.

The standard fate line tends to start at the base of the palm in the middle. There are variations however that may come swooping in from the thumb side or pinkie side of the base of the palm.

This line has a time line. As we did when we were looking at marriage lines, we take the basic lifespan from the life expectancy indicated by the life line. We then project that amount of time on the space from the base of the palm (top of the bracelets) up to the base of the middle finger.

This gives us a way to figure out what happens when...

In looking at this time line, the base of the palm is the birth end of the fate line and the finger end of the palm is the death end of it.

As this line flows up the palm, you may see forks leading into it (branches that connect with the primary line going upwards). You may see forks coming out of it (branches splitting off as the line goes upwards). You may even see a parallel line that is not one of the other major lines (a double fate line, although this is very rare.).

If the fate line doesn't look exactly as it does on the picture, don't worry. There are lots of legitimate variations. Just remember, if you've got a complicated fate line situation, you can always find it by starting at the end. Spot the line that ends under the middle finger and see where it comes from.

That's the fate line.

As I said above, the fate line stands for luck and money. The deeper the line, the more luck and the more money there is.

Please note that how much is "more" is relative.

For some people, when it comes to money, the world is not enough. For such folks, a sickly fate line might mean they were down to their last million.

For other folks, true wealth is "a loaf of bread, a jug of wine, and thou singing beside me in the wilderness". For them, a "rich" fate line might indicate a considerably smaller number than the same type of line for people in the first group.

When speaking of money, I tend not to mention specific amounts unless I really need to. Instead, I'll describe a standard good quality fate line as "enough to pay your bills, pursue your goals, have some fun and help other people, too-and what could be finer than that?"

It's worth noting that the fate line is about both money and luck (the ability to take chances and come up smelling like a rose).How do you tell how much is luck and how much money?

This is not that hard actually. All you need to do is revisit your old friends, the bracelets. If you recall, the middle bracelet stands for wealth and wealth alone.

Compare that bracelet with your fate line. What do you see?

If the bracelet is light and the fate line dark, this person is Fortune's Child and what they risk, they will likely achieve, but there won't be much brass in their pockets. (They'll probably be lucky enough for someone to treat them to a drink however...).

If both are light, this person will have to be clever with his resources and not take foolish risks. What he has, he will have earned as opposed to fallen into.

If both are dark, the money will be there and the luck is determined by trial and error. (Some say the rich can buy good fortune. I don't know as I agree with that, though...).

Next time, we'll look at what the fate line tells us about work and money throughout our lives.

. <u>Hand Notes</u>

If you're going to be reading a lot of palms, one thing that's good to carry with you is hand sanitizer.

Not only does it help deal with germs (your own or those of others), but it also works well as a symbolic way to separate from the energy of your querant at the end of a reading or to clear negative energy, if this is needed.

Chapter Twenty-Six

Fate Line II -
Working for a Living

In the last chapter, we shook hands with the fate line and examined the basics of how it indicates luck and money in a querant's life. This chapter, we're going to get more specific about what a fate line (and other markings) can tell us about the querant's job and career.

When doing readings, the two areas that people most want to know about are love, and money/job.

For love, you'll look at the marriage lines to identify significant people in their lives; and at the heart line to determine how ready (or unready) they are to be in a relationship.

For money and job, we start at the fate line.

As noted previously, the fate line starts (at birth) at the base of the palm and flows upwards to end under the middle finger, or finger of Saturn. (This point is the end of life). Using the life expectancy that we obtained at our life line, we can locate any period in a person's life on their fate line in order to figure out what's going on at that time of a monetary/material nature.

Following the path of bottom to top, any branches that flow upwards and merge with the fate line tend to indicate multiple sources of income, bearing fruit at the point(s) in time that they are visible. Windfalls and inheritances are two examples of such largess.

Any branches that separate and run upwards from the fate line tend to indicate periods when one is trying out several ways of bringing in income. One example would be having two different jobs. This usually (but not always) is a temporary situation and resolves by the querant picking one path or the other. Sometimes, however, it becomes a long-term or permanent arrangement. It's good in these cases to be sure the querants remember to maintain balance in their lives between work and other important aspects, such as love, family, fun, growth,etc. If they do, experimenting is fine.

The deeper the line is at any point, the more money/prosperity there is at that point in time. The lighter the line is, the less money.

Retirement tends to hit around the point where the fate line crosses the head line (but not always. This point on the palm is a specific point in time and some folks retire earlier in life or later). It's not surprising that, for a majority of folks, the fate line gets lighter at this point. (You don't need a psychic to tell you that you may have less income after you retire...)

Surprisingly enough, for some people, the fate line gets darker once they hit retirement. (Once they're free to follow their dreams, they actually find something to do that they love that makes them more money!)

Your standard fate line starts in the middle of the base of the palm. This is your basic "job" job - a way of making money with no unusual influences.

You may like it.

You may tolerate it.

You may tough your way through it.

It's a job...

If your fate line curves in from the thumb side of the base of the palm, from inside of the life line, it means that your family has a strong influence on how you make your money.

It may be a family allowance or inheritance.

It may be being in the family business.

It may be having a career that's traditional in your family. (Ex:"Mom's a cop, Dad's a cop and I'm a cop, too!").

It may be doing something in keeping with your family's values (as opposed to Family Values, which are something totally different....).

It may be doing something that is completely opposed to your family's values, just because it bothers them. (This is more common for folks with changeling marks).

The bottom line is that your family will have a strong influence on what you do to make a living.

If your fate line swoops in from the mound on the pinkie side of the base of your palm (the mound of the Moon), your source of income will be either creative or intuitive or both.

You may have a standard creative job, like ballerina or architect.

You may have a regular job and do it creatively, like Ben and Jerry did with ice cream.

You may have a standard intuitive job, like being a palm reader like me.

You may have a regular job and bring intuition into it, like the guy who picks stocks based on his hunches, or the psychoanalyst, who steers the direction of counseling based on her instincts.

The bottom line is that, when you bring creativity and/or intuition into the workplace, that's when you prosper the most.

Now, let's go to some of the markings...

A break in the fate line indicates a change of jobs, or a change of careers, depending on how big the break is.

Sometimes, you'll see a break where the two lines run side by side for awhile, and then the original line fades out and the new one continues on. This often indicates someone starting their own business and continuing to work their day job while they build up business in their company.

If the break is surrounded by a square, there is extra special protection during the transition.

An island can indicate being stuck in a dead-end job (or working in one of those catalog phone centers run in jails, I suppose...)

A cross on the fate line indicates conflict. Check to see who's likely to win.

A star or asterix indicates something unusually good in the financial arena. (Winning the lotto would be one example. Check the depth of the fate line following this point to determine if the querant wins big. Does the fate line go very deep, then lighter again shortly thereafter? Easy come, easy go.)

A triangle would indicate special good luck or good fortune. You start producing what-cha-ma-callits just as everyone decides they need one. Your paintings become a hit and sell like hot cakes. You are the golden child. (Remember that this only lasts for the time covered by the triangle).

And so forth....

Money tends to surge and ebb like the tide for most people. (I know it has in my life at times...) When reading the fate line, it's good to cue your client in on when to expect leaner times, and when to expect more prosperity. This gives them the opportunity to fiscally plan wisely, to put a bit away when there are challenging times coming, and overall to have a better life. Give them the info they need to make good choices.

It's also good to let them know when changes in job or employment are in the offing.

And always remind them about free will.

Since we've been talking about joys and careers, the next chapter will be a brief overview on some other places in the palm you can go for information on the subject.

Chapter Twenty-Seven

On the Job Training

The two most frequent areas of concern I'm asked about in a palm reading are love and money/job/career. Under the topic of job, you'll get questions such as:

1) Will I keep my job?
2) Should I change careers?
3) What field should I go into?
4) Is this sideline I'm working on going to be profitable?
5) How can I prosper more fully?

And so forth....

For the last two chapters, we've been looking at the fate line, which covers luck, money and, by extension, career. Since we've been discussing careers and jobs, let's take a quick look at other places in the palm where information about the workplace can be found.

Some of the areas we'll be reviewing are ones you're already familiar with. Some of them are areas we've yet to explore - I'll mention them briefly to put them in this context, and you'll learn more about them when we get to them later in this book.

Many of these areas cover skills and strengths that can affect a person's job choice and performance. By alerting your client, he knows what he needs to emphasize for better success on the job.

Looking at the head line
Is this person organized?
Logical?
Creative? Is he an idea person?
Will he need structure to work or is he more free flow?
Is he a thinker?
Does he learn new things easily?
Would a job with less thinking and more action suit him

better?

> The heart line-
> How are her people skills?
> Does she do better on a team or solo?
> Does she work and play nicely with others?
> Is she stressed? Does she need to do something about this?
> Does she like drama? Does she create it?
> The fame line (ends under ring finger - in upcoming chapter)
> Will he be in the public eye?
> The health line (ends under the pinkie - in upcoming chapter)
> How's her health and energy?
> Are health care benefits particularly important to her?
> Does she need set hours?

> On to the mounds (in upcoming chapters).....
> Jupiter (under index finger)-
> Is he self-motivated?
> Does he have good self-esteem, supporting sound decisions?
> Does he have leadership ability?
> Saturn (under middle finger)-
> Is she responsible?
> A team player?
> Does she overextend herself?
> Does she know how to say no?
> Does she have a good grasp of how much she can reasonably accomplish?
> Apollo (under ring finger)-
> Does he have skills in the Arts or Sciences?
> Mercury (under pinkie)
> Does she have skills in making things run efficiently and effectively?
> Is she good at making money?

Is she a good communicator?

Does she have a good head for business?

Medical Stigmata (vertical marks on mound of Mercury)-

Is she a healer?

Is she in a healing or related human services helping career?

If not, has she considered this?

Venus (base of thumb)

Does he love beautiful things?

Does he have developed senses (such as a great sense of taste for a chef)?

Is he aesthetic?

Is he very sensual?

Luna or the Moon (heel of hand on the pinkie side)-

Is she creative?

Is she intuitive?

Can she trust her instincts?

Does she?

Is she psychic?

Mars (midpoint on each side of the hand)

Does he love excitement?

Is he a thrill seeker?

Is his job exciting enough for him?

How much risk is acceptable to him?

Does she stand up for what she believes in?

Is she afraid of confrontation?

And our good friend, the thumb-

How flexible is he?

Does he need set hours or can he adjust?

Can he hang in for the long haul?

Can he handle it when times get tough?

The shapes of the palms and fingers can also give us useful information about our querant's basic personality and therefore what type of work would suit him or her better. While one can try anything, it's good to play to your strengths.

This gives you a few ideas of where to look to answer questions your querant may have in regards to career.

Next, we'll go on to renown and recognition...

Chapter Twenty-Eight

The Fame Line -
May We Have Your Autograph?

The next line in our cavalcade of landmarks is the fame line. The fame line stands for (wait for it!...) Fame. Renown. Infamy. Being widely known for who you are or what you've done.

So, let's go take a look at the road to stardom.....

To locate the fame line, let's turn again to Figure 6, "Fate, Fame and Health Lines". The fame line is a diagonal, vertical line (labeled "B") that starts at the bottom or wrist end of the palm and runs upwards towards the ring finger.

Like the fate line, the fame line has a time line. The bottom of the palm is birth and the base of the ring finger is the end of life. As we've done on previous lines, you take the life expectancy you determined on the life line and project it into the space covered by the fame line, letting you know when fame will come into (or pass out of) your querant's life and when his life will be more private.

Now, as you might by now extrapolate, the deeper the fame line is at any point through life, the more well-known the person is at that time. The lighter the line is, the less well-known.

Therefore, a fame line as deep as the Grand Canyon indicates a mega-star.

A moderately deep fame line is someone who's not on the cover of a popular magazine, but is widely known for something they've done amongst many people who've never met them. (The analogy that I like is saying ""You need information on an event and call a stranger to get it. You say "Hello, I'm Ms. Hardwork..." and the person at the other end of the line gasps "You're Ms. Hardwork ! I've really wanted to meet you!", "I admire what you've been doing very much!" , calls out to someone else at their end of the line saying "You'll never guess who I'm talking to!..." or other similar responses.")

A light line or no line indicates relative obscurity or privacy (dependant on how you chose to view it).

It's worthy of note that a fame line can equally indicate fame (being well-known for something good) or infamy (being well-known for something not so good....

Therefore it doesn't pass judgment. It just registers how well-known you are.

So, for folks with active fame lines, it's good to advise them to be sure to be ready for their lives to be an open book for the period of time when fame is indicated.

Because they will be....

And, as for additional landmarks on the fame line,.....

Branches coming in from different parts of the palm can indicate different causes of fame.

Branches coming off of the fame line can indicate fame in multiple areas. (This is a subtle, but noteworthy, distinction from the branches coming in.).

A star or asterix indicates fame as a result of a positive unusual event.

A break in a fame line indicates a period of withdrawal followed by a "come back".

A triangle indicates the winds of fortune supporting your renown.

A cross or "X" indicates a very public rivalry.

And, so forth, ...

When reading the fame line, it's a grand idea to ask the person first if they want to be famous. Many do not, and are relieved if there is little or no renown in their hand.

If there's no fame there, tell them. If there is some, remind them to watch what they say and do because there are points where their lives will be on display.

Some folks, on the other hand, are looking for fame. Many (but not all) of these tend to be young people (athletes, rock stars, nuclear physicists, to name a few), who hope to excel in their chosen field sufficiently enough that they will stand out from others.

There's nothing wrong with hungering for stand-out excellence.

If there's fame in their palm, pat them on the back and tell them. If there's no fame, I usually say I'm sorry and whisper to them that the current President would probably gladly trade places with them at this point. (This helps them to laugh and relax enough to think about how to change things.)

In either case, if what's in the hand is not what that person wants, it only means that, if they continue to do things the way they've been doing them, this is the result. Remind them about free will and encourage them to explore their alternative choices which can create a life that is more of what they want.

This concludes our tour of the fame line. Next stop, health....

<u>Hand Notes</u>

It's interesting to me to find that different readers tend to attract different kinds of palms. For instance, a large majority of the folks I see have round palms (something you'll be learning about in chapter 31), whereas a friend of mine who reads palms sees far more folks with square palms, and my most active student sees mostly spatulate palms.

Now, if this were a question of repeat clients, I'd chalk it up to individual tastes, but the truth is that these patterns are consistent with first time clients as well as repeat querants.

I can only assume that there is something non-tangible that attracts the right client to that right psychic.

I find that both remarkable and comforting, actually...

Chapter Twenty-Nine

Health Line -
Physician, Heal Thyself!

We've learned about the fate line. We've learned about the fame line. Now it's time to review the third of the secondary lines of the palm - the health line.

As previously noted, love and money tie for the most frequent concerns for people getting a palm reading. Health tends to be a close runner-up, although still not as frequent as love or money. Because of this, this line is a key part of most readings.

The health line tells us about the querant's health. It covers not only physical health, but also health in mind, and spirit.

Let's start by locating your health line...

Before we locate the health line, you need to know about a curious phenomenon that is unique to it.

In most lines, as you know, the darker a line is, the more of the characteristic associated with that line you have. The lighter the line, the less you have.

The health line is different......

There are three different types of health line based on darkness/lightness (And there are individual variations within these types; however we're just going to stick with the three basic types...) These are dark health lines, light health lines, and no health lines. Your health line can also vary between the types based on your level of health at any particular time in your life.

But they're not what you would expect, based on everything you've learned before this...

Some people can eat anything, drink anything, stay up all night and don't get sick unless you hit them in the head with a hammer.

These maximally healthy people **have no health lines!!!**

That's right. Read it again if you need to. No health lines.

The next step downwards are people that have some health problems but are managing them well. Their health issues affect their lives (because of the adaptations that they need to make things work), but do not significantly limit them.

These people have dark/deep health lines.

The third type of the health line is the light line. People with light health lines have significant health problems having significant impact on their lives, and may require a lot of energy, focus and/or adaptations to make their lives work.

To review:

Highest stage - No health line/amazingly healthy

Middle Stage - Dark Health Line/moderately healthy - managing any issues

Lowest Stage - Light Health line/significant medical issues, either not under control or managing the impact of health on life takes major work.

It's worth noting that sometimes you will encounter someone with a major health condition (for example, diabetes, cancer, a stroke, etc) whose health line looks better/is at a higher level than you would expect, given their situation. This is a person who is so effective at managing the impact of their condition on the rest of their life that it's almost effortless or automatic.

Like that medical condition doesn't exist....

Got all of this? Let's look for our health lines.....

To locate the health line, we go once more to Figure 6, "Fate, Fame and Health Lines". The health line is a diagonal, vertical line (labeled "C") that starts at the bottom, or wrist end of the palm and runs upwards towards the pinkie. (As noted above, there may be sections of the palm, where there is actually no line apparent during times when the Querant is very healthy. Even where there is no line visible, the above description details where to look for the health line or lack thereof.).

Like fate and fame lines before, the health line has a time line. The wrist or base of the palm is birth. The base of the pinkie is the end of life. Take that life expectancy from the life line (which you are very familiar with by now) and project it on this space. Now you can locate when in life your querant's health will be good and when it will be more challenging.

The health line is not just unique in its interpretation of what dark/light/no lines mean. It's also got a special twist in regards to interpretation of dominant and non-dominant hands.

As previously noted, your non-dominant hand indicates the potential you were born with. The dominant hand indicates what you're doing with it. In the health line, there's a bit more to this.

On the health line, the non-dominant hand tends to also indicate the health potential you got from your family. This includes both our genetic load and the things our family taught us (intentionally or not) about health and things that affect our health.

Like how to eat.

Or how active to be.

Or how to handle stress.

The dominant hand tells us how our health is as of this point, both now and in the future. So both the choices we've made and the things we may not have chosen but that have inadvertently come into our lives cause our health lines to change from what was in our non-dominant hand.

To give an example, if your parents were non-smokers and you chose to start smoking, it can change the type of health line in your dominant hand, so it differs from the non-dominant one.

For this reason, this is one area where it is particularly important to compare non-dominant and dominant hands. Because of our good friend Free Will, if a querant has health problems, he can take steps to change this (and if your querant is successful, his line will change to reflect this). Comparing hands can give you information about this.

If a problem is noted in both hands, this is something that may have a genetic or long-term habit basis for this issue. This will probably (but not always) be harder to change - but not impossible!

If a problem is in the dominant but not the non-dominant, it can be easier to change, as it is less locked in.

If the problem is in the non-dominant hand but not the dominant one, this person was originally slotted for health issues, but has made such good choices that he or she has already overcome them. Pat this person on the back and tell him or her to keep it up!

This gives you a basic grounding in the health line. More health line info next chapter.

Chapter Thirty

Health Line II -
Body, Mind, and Spirit

In our last chapter, we began to look at the health line. We located it on the palm. We talked about the differences in light, dark and no health lines. We looked at the unique aspects in comparing the health line in both hands, learning what health comes from our family and what from our own choices and experiences.

Now, let's get more in depth on the issues of health.

Now if you've got someone with a dark or light health line, this is definitely a person with health issues.

Sometimes, this will be a surprise to your querants (and possibly a clue to go get themselves checked out...). Some may even not believe you.

In such readings, I may give information that the querant is unaware of and disbelieves. In these cases, usually I'll see the person again in the future. He'll tell me he didn't believe me at the time, but that later something had popped up to show that the reading was indeed accurate.

For some people, although they don't buy it, the reading causes them to get a check-up resulting in catching a condition early...

Many times, you'll be telling him something he already knows.

You can tell him if the health issues are familial or brought on by his own choices and experiences. This may also be something he knows.

By themselves, these are things that may make you look good as a reader, but have limited use to your querant in making a better life.

So what can you tell a querant in this area that empowers him, rather than simply confirming that you are a good reader?

You can tell him about Free Will and that he has the ability to change his fate. That's a good start on the path to personal empowerment. You can also take it a bit further.

I find many times (but not always) that, besides the health issues indicated by this line, you'll also find an overdeveloped mound of Saturn. We'll learn about Saturn later in the book, however, to give you the basic health implications at this juncture, an overdeveloped mound of Saturn indicates someone who's so very over-responsible that they are invariably too busy taking care of everyone around them to take care of themselves...

There are a number of ways that this plays out. Sometimes the querant knows that he needs to do something healthy for himself (for example: exercise), but never finds time because he's too busy caring for the needs of others. Sometimes he engages in unhealthy practices (ex: overdoing fast food), because it frees up more time to help others. Sometimes, he's neglected his own well-being so much that his body will actually create a real illness because it's the only way to get him to do caring things for himself. (For example, chronic fatigue syndrome can be Nature's way of saying "Slow down or fall down...")

You may need to talk to this person about balance, about treating himself as least as nicely as he does other people. I find that many times it's helpful to explain that, if he burns himself out, he can't help anyone; however, if he takes care of himself, he's stronger and healthier and can therefore help more other folks. This makes this response a "win-win" (and puts it in terms that a chronic helper will more possibly resonate with, use and benefit from).

For anyone with problems indicated in his health lines, I like to advise him that he needs to find what keeps him healthy in body, mind and spirit.

Some things may be mainstream medicine.

Some of these may be alternative medicine (such as chiropractic treatments or Reiki).

Some of them may not even be medicine as we usually think of it.

Like turning up the volume on the car radio and singing along at the top of your lungs, because it feels great and boosts your endorphins; which is good for the immune system.

Or spending time in Nature, because it calms you down and drops your blood pressure.

I advise folks to take advice from experts but to be the final arbitrator on what works for them as individuals, rather than as members of a demographic group.

Finally, I tell them that, once they've found what works for them, they need to make time to do it on a regular basis. This can be hard for most of us, and especially for the overly-responsible folks we talked about earlier in this chapter.

It's worth a reminder that the health line is health, not just in the body, but also in mind, and spirit. While the distinction is not always clear-cut, there are some indicators.

If there's a problem in the health line and a steeply sloping head line, the problem may be mental.

Be cautious in interpreting it this way though. With chronic health problems, many times depression can set in (which would also look like this).

If there are chains on the heart line, it can indicate a stress or emotional component.

If there's a star or asterix on the life line (remember, on the life line, this is a crisis) at one point in time and, at the same point in time on the health line, the line gets worse, this can indicate some kind of accident or traumatic illness with long range effects (a stroke, for instance).

A point in time when the life line gets lighter and the health line gets worse can indicate a health problem that drains you of energy.

If there are more specific health questions, towards the end of this book, I'll be teaching you some other supportive methods of divination that can supplement a palm reading and give you additional specifics.

When looking at health, the primary place to look is on the health line; however, as is true with other areas of concern, it's always a good idea to look at other landmarks on the palm in order to see what other indicators may be found.

This concludes our tour of the health line and the area of health. Next time, we move on to the structure of the hand...

Figure 7 – Shape of Palms

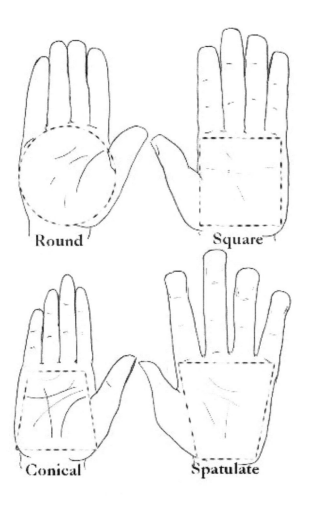

Figure 7 – Shape of Palms

<u>Hand Notes</u>

The two primary reasons that people get readings are to find out about love or prosperity/career. Health questions come very closely behind these other two topics.

One useful concept to note is that Reiki or other kinds of energy work for promoting health combine easily with palmistry.

It is inappropriate, of course, to use these techniques without your client's permission. If you have this permission and you chose to, however, it's very easy to run Reiki while holding a client's hands during a reading.

Chapter Thirty-One

The Shape of the Palm-
And How to See It

Having completed the primary and secondary lines of the palm (along with a number of other landmarks making up the basic palm reading), now it's time to move on to more structural features of the palm. Let's start with the shape of the palm.....

In most palmistry books, they'll refer to different "types" of hands. They'll speak of a "psychic" type; or a "philosophic" type; or many other types. Each type has, as part of its definition, a specific combination of palm shape and finger shape.

At the end of the section on "hand types", there's invariably a little one sentence throw-away which says "Occasionally, you may see a hand which is a mixture of these types"...

Or something to that effect.

Well, I've been reading palms for approximately 40 years now, and I've yet to see a palm that wasn't a so-called "mixed palm".

In practice, I've found this concept of hand types not very useful or applicable.

Which is why I use a different method.

I tend to look at the shape of the palm and the shape of the fingers individually. The way I see it is that the shape of the palm is the person's primary personality, and the shape of the fingers modifies it (kind of like how the Sun sign and the Ascendant work in astrology). This has proven to give an accurate reflection of the person in question (and is also useful in casual contact with people....).

If you want to learn and use the "types" of palms, feel free; but you'll have to go out and learn them elsewhere. (Go, with my blessings! Come back afterwards, if you like...) Even if you wish to look into types of palms, you may want to cruise this lesson, and the one on finger shape first. Historically, one of the things folks find the most challenging in reading palms is determining the shape of the palms and I've tried to make it clear and easy for you here.

The basics having been laid, let's go look at the shape of the palm...

Before we start, you'll need Figure 7, "Shapes of Hands/Palms" as a reference. Set this page where you can see it easily without holding it or moving to see it, as both of your hands will be engaged positioning the hand to look at the shape of the palm.

Most times, you'll be seated facing your querant. Take his hand that you're going to look at in your outside hand (the one that can grasp it from the thumb side when the hand is palm up). For his right hand, you'll be holding it in your left; for is left hand, in your right, if you are seated facing him.

Gently turn the palm over, turning towards the thumb until the palm is up, and as level as it can go.

Watch your querant's face closely as you do this. Some people's hands can turn all the way over, while others can only go part way. The further over you can get it, the easier it will be for you to read. The priority, however, is to avoid causing pain for your querant, so you turn within their tolerance. His facial expression will tell you if you're turning too far.

To restate this - **you turn as far as the client can tolerate and no farther.**

Don't hurt your client.

Now that you've got the hand palm up, hold it in the hand you turned with. Use your other hand to grasp the tip of his thumb, and move it until it is even with and above the index finger side of the palm.

In other words, put the thumb in neutral.

Why do we do this? If the thumb is out to the side, it can distort the shape of the palm, concealing its true shape.

So you put the thumb in neutral.....

And the shape of the palm appears.....

The basic palm shapes fall into four varieties:

Square.

Round.

Conical (like a cone).

And spatulate (based on the shape of a spade. Those wacky Ancients! They must have been using some pretty odd looking shovels...).

The square palm is basically square. Equally wide at both ends, and in the middle. It also tends to be roughly the same height, and width.

The round palm is widest at the middle, and narrower at both ends.

The conical hand is widest at the wrist end, and tapers to narrowest at the base of the fingers.

And the spatulate hand is narrowest at the wrist, and tapers outwards to widest at the base of the fingers.

Many times, once you've got the hand in position, you'll find that it's relatively easy to determine the shape of the palm by looking.

Sometimes, though, it's a close call and you may want to measure dimensions. Some folks use a ruler. I tend to measure a dimension by positioning my thumb and forefinger at either end of the palm, then moving the whole "pinch" to compare with the other sections of the palm.

You need to do what works for you. Whatever gets you there is good, (as long as no one gets hurt and you don't alarm the horses...)

Now you've got the knowledge you need to determine the shape of the palm. Next time, we'll go into what each shape means.

<u>Hand Notes</u>

When doing readings, you're going to spend a lot of time holding people's hands. This is a lot more pleasant for all concerned if your hands are not rough and dry. A good hand lotion or balm can help with this.

When picking out a lotion, keep in mind that many people have allergies that can be triggered by scent. I find that fruit scents are less likely to stimulate peoples' allergies, but that is still far from certain. The safest bet is a lotion that's free of scent.

That being said, it's also important to choose something that makes you happy to use. Not only will you use it more frequently if it pleases you, but also any way to incorporate happiness in your life, even if only in small amounts, is certainly worth doing.

A sample size which travels with you, also increases the chances of you nurturing your hands and therefore those of others.

Chapter Thirty-Two
The Shape of the Palm
The Shape of Yourself

In the last chapter, we looked at the philosophy of "types" of palms, the "mixed" palm, and an alternative approach utilizing the shape of the palms and the fingers. We discussed how to position the hand to look at the shape of the palm, and how to determine palm shape.

Now that you know what shape the palm you're looking at is, it's time to look at what that shape means....

The square palm is square - roughly equal across at all points from top to bottom (or, if you prefer, bottom to top...) of the palm, and usually the same up and down as well.

The square palm personality is basically...well... square. Square palm people are very grounded and practical. They're usually logical, efficient and organized. (If they seem disorganized, it's usually because they have an organizational system uniquely their own that works perfectly for them).

These are the people you want fixing your car, repairing your house, and other such responsibilities. They'll do the job well, on time, with no drama and at reasonable costs.

In love, square palm folks don't say "I love you" frequently. Instead, they'll make you soup when you're sick, tune up your car's brakes so you're safe and drive 300 miles at 2 a.m. to pick you up if your car dies. With them, they say "I love you" in actions, not words.

Square palm people believe in what they can see and touch. For this reason, they often don't believe in psychic phenomenon.

In particular, if I've got someone with square palms and corresponding square fingers sitting with me, I can predict without using any psychic ability at all that this person is sitting in my chair because their boyfriend/girlfriend/husband/wife has sat them there saying "You're going to get a reading, and I'm going to pay for it!".

Invariably, in these situations, the square palm person is polite and a delight to read for. I particularly enjoy it because, almost always, at some point in the reading (usually the thumb, for some reason...), something I say will resonate with the square querant, and I can see the "click" as he realizes that this is a real experience, not just fluff or theater.

When I see that "click", I give him a couple of seconds to process. (after all, his view of the world has just gotten bigger...), then proceed. Sometimes, he'll say to me "Hey! This is real, isn't it?" I'll smile and say "Yes. Do you want me to go on?" He'll invariably say yes.

Square palms don't believe in readings until they get proof, but you don't have to shove it down their throats. Once they have their evidence, they smoothly modify their worldview to accommodate the world of psychic phenomena in a way that is a delight.

The round palm is narrower at the top and bottom and wider in the middle.

People with round palms are feeling people; loving, caring, emotional in good and/or in bad ways. They love people and care about them. They may be vulnerable to sacrificing themselves to the needs of others. They're good with people, good with communications and charm and working as a team. They're good listeners. They like to talk about feelings.

When it comes to love, while the square palm person will make you soup and bring it to you when you're sick, the round palms person will feed it to you if you need help, and wipe your forehead with a cool cloth. The round palm person will also say "I love you." A lot.

The round palm person is often vulnerable to letting people take advantage of her. She is sometimes so nice that she forgets how to say "No". She needs good boundaries, so she can help others without letting them walk all over her. To determine the state of her boundaries, you'll be looking at the mound of Saturn (which we'll cover in more detail later in this book).

The round palm person also has a vulnerability to spending so much time taking care of the needs of others that she forgets to take care of herself. To find out whether your querant has good balance in self care/other care, you'll also be looking at Saturn.

The round palm person wants to help people and save them from harm. She wants to protect people so much that sometimes she forgets that people have Free Will.

Sometimes people don't want to listen to the round palm, even though they'd be smart to do so. Sometimes they want to do the dumb thing or eat the junk food. Sometimes people create crises for themselves because crisis can be a powerful teacher. If this is the case, we don't always do them a favor by taking their crisis away from them, as they may feel the need to create a **bigger** crisis.

Sometimes, people need to learn things the hard way.

And, though that's dumb as dirt, if that's their choice, we need to respect that

The round palm person may need the reminder that she can offer help and advice, but that she can't help someone who doesn't want to be helped. Can't save someone who doesn't want to be saved.

Good boundaries are a two-way arrangement.

The round palm often needs to be reminded that, if she's done the best she could, that's all she could do. If the other person refused help and then went through a painful process in consequence, the round palm will tend to feel guilty; but if she did all she could do, that was all she could do.

At that point, angst is a waste of energy....

Energy that could be used for something beneficial.....

Like helping someone who wants help....

Or even (heaven forbid!) doing something nice for one's self.

The conical palm is widest at the base (the wrist end) and tapers to narrowest at the base of the fingers.

The conical palm person is a dreamer, a visionary. He tends to have big ideas that can change the world, but is poorly grounded and, unless he has other moderating features, (such as the ever-popular thumb chain), that off-set his basic palm, he may have a lot of problems finishing things.

Conical palm people are wonderful people, but may need a lot of support and maintenance from others.

In love, the conical palm person may make extravagant gestures of love like no other lover has through history....

Or he may forget your birthday.

In a relationship, the conical palm person should probably not be in charge of the checkbook....

The conical person needs to work on focus, on making dreams come into reality, and on practical factors in life.

I rarely see people with this type of palm.

The spatulate palm is narrowest at the base/wrist end, and tapers outwards to widest at the base of the fingers. It was called "spatulate" because the ancients thought it looked like a spade or shovel.

The spatulate palm person is a maker or creator, a person who moves into a space and makes it her own and, when she moves on, there is something there that wasn't there before because she has "made it so" (to paraphrase a certain space epic).

This something may be something concrete, such as a building or a painting, or something more abstract, such as a philosophy or a revolution.

Artists have this hand, and artisans, and inventors, and explorers, and scientists (mad or no....).

In love, the spatulate hand will come up with amazing ways to tell you she cares. She'll tend to let her actions do the talking.

Things to check on a spatulate palm-

Thumb chain-for the "stick-to-it-niveness" to make things happen.

Finger shapes - without a certain amount of moderating round/people factor in the fingers, a spatulate palm can be ruthless in pursuit of her dreams. With it, she works and plays nicely with others (and can even get them to help).

Conical fingers can contribute good ideas to make real.

It's worth reemphasizing that, as people change the direction of their lives, their palms change to reflect their new selves and new futures. Believe it or not, this even applies to the shape of palms. The actual hand shape can change, dependant on who you are and where you're going in life.

Well, there are the basics on the shapes of palms and the personalities that go with them. Next chapter, we'll look at the shape of fingers.

Figure 8 – the Shape of Fingers

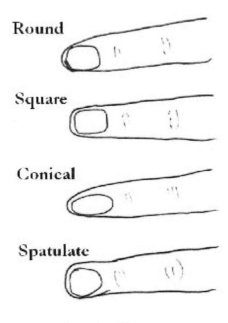

Figure 8 – the Shape of Fingers

Chapter Thirty – Three
The Shape of the Fingers -
The Nuances of Personality

In our last two chapters, we learned how the shape of our palms indicates the basic nature of our personalities. As previously noted, the shape of the tips of our fingers adjust and modify that basic personality, much as the ascendant modifies the influence of your sun sign in astrology. Let's look at these fingertips in more detail now.....

As a visual reference to studying finger shapes, please look at Figure 8, "Shapes of Fingers". This will help as we discuss different shapes.

It is worthy of note that often people will have more than one shape of fingers on a hand. Indeed, a majority of the people I read have not only "mixed" type hands, but also a mixture of types of fingers as well.

The round finger tip can be usually even rounder than it is pictured as the first fingertip on the illustration. It is notable because it only begins to taper inwards at the very tip of the finger. It always looks to me like one half of a tiny little coin...

Round finger energy is loving, caring people energy. Round finger tips bring both concern for others, and the ability to work and play nicely with others into the mix.

The square finger (the second pictured) is almost flat across the tip.

The energy of square finger tips is (as you may have guessed) square. It's grounded and practical. It sees things in black and white, and believes in what it can see and touch and experience.

The conical fingertip (the third finger pictured) is conical or pointed. It tapers towards the tip, but it starts tapering considerably further from the tip than your round fingertip does.

The energy of the conical fingertips is visionary, idealist energy - the energy of someone who sees things not as they are but as they could be. While a conical palm can be brilliant but impractical, conical fingers combined with other aspects (such as a round or spatulate palm) can be the fingers of someone who will change the world....

The spatulate fingertip (the fourth pictured) is also flattish like the square fingertip; however it differs from a square fingertip in that it bulges out at the sides. It looks kind of like a little mushroom.

The energy of spatulate fingertips is creative, in every sense of the word. This is a finger that does things and makes things happen.

As you may have noticed, the meaning of the shapes of fingertips echoes the meaning of the shape of the palm. Consider this to be like a personality milkshake - the shape of the palm is the milk/primary ingredient or flavor, and the shape of the fingertips is like an added flavor that modifies the overall effect.

So let's look at some examples of how these combinations might work out.

A person with square palms and square fingertips is extremely grounded, almost to the pocket protector level.

A person with round palms and conical fingers is an idealist who wants what's best for people. This person may have a tendency to meddle but will also help people.

A person with spatulate palms and pointed fingertips has brilliant ideas, and the ability to make them real. Throw in a round fingertip or two, and everybody wants to jump on their bandwagon ("Come on guys! Let's put on a show! My father has a barn!...)

Do you see how this works?

Here's a chance to have some fun. Try naming a shape of palm; add on one or more shapes of fingers (you may chose up to four, although I don't remember ever seeing more than three different shapes on one hand....); and see if you can figure out what kind of person this would be.

(Give your head line a work-out; extrapolate a little...)

Well, there's the basics for the shapes of fingers. Next time, we move on to an introduction to the mounds (the "boomps") on your hands.

Figure 9 - Mounds

A – Venus
B – Jupiter
C – Saturn
D – Apollo
E – Mercury
F – the Moon
G1 and G2 – Mars

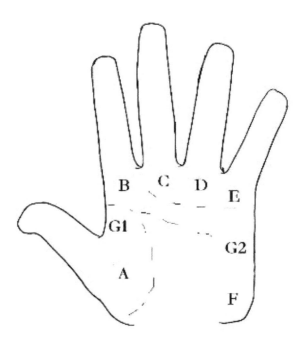

Figure 9 – Mounds

Chapter Thirty-Four
Meet the Mounds

Having gone through the primary and secondary lines of the hand, the shape of palms and fingers, and an assortment of other features, it's now time to move on to more structural formations of the palms. We're going to look at the bumps on the palm, which are called "mounds".

If you may recall, in earlier chapters I've referred to the difference between your dominant and non-dominant hand; how the non-dominant hand tells us about the potential you were born with, and the dominant, what you're doing with it. I told you that there are certain features where it may be useful to compare palms.

This can tell you of unrealized talent. This can tell you of where a querant has worked hard and, through his own good effort, has moved beyond his natural talents to become so much more. This can tell you about traumatic events that have thrown your client off-track, wounds that need to heal, limits that need to be addressed...

Just to name a few things.....

I find that the mounds are an area where it's particularly useful to compare hands, for all the information that it can bring you.

When reading the mounds, or any time you're going to spend significant amounts of time comparing both hands, you'll be spending a noticeable amount of time holding both of your querant's hands in a somewhat locked-in position. At this point, ergonomics (otherwise known as good positioning) becomes important.

I tend to do this kind of reading facing the client across a table. To prevent back strain on either of you, you need to look at several factors.

Since you'll be holding one position for some time, you'll

probably end up with your elbows propped on the table. At this point, it's important to have a table that's the right height so you don't end up hunched over.

If you're hunched, you'll get lost in the reading, and not realize what else is happening until you finish, try to straighten up, and can't...

You need to be sitting so your arms are reaching to each other without having to stretch noticeably. This means that your table needs to be narrow enough to facilitate this, or you both have to be sitting close enough to the table, or both. If you don't, you both risk pain in your shoulders, neck, or back.

I like to encourage clients to "scoot up" to the table before we start a reading, to prevent any uncomfortable positioning.

If you or your querant are hunched or stretched, you'll get uncomfortable as the reading progresses. This will detract from the reading. It'll also hurt, and can have a more serious impact on those who already have problems, such as neck or back pain.

It's better to think about positioning before you start, than suffer because you didn't....

In the lines, we looked at the depth or lightness of the line, for an indication of how much of the characteristic covered by that line your querant had.

The mounds are a little different. You're going to be looking at how large, and how muscular a mound is in order to determine the amount of the specified characteristic.

Mounds are kind of like the three bears. In most of them, it's possible to be "too big" (having too much of the characteristic), "too small"(having too little of the characteristic), or "just right"....

Furthermore, mounds can be deceptive. A mound can look big and muscular, but when you touch it, it's full of hot air and collapses like a cheap soufflé.

For instance, one mound covers self-esteem. A collapsing

mound in this position indicates someone who looks like he believes in himself, but (in reality) has poor self-esteem, and puts on a false front.(Sound like anyone you know?)

Because of this, I find it to be important to not just look at the mounds, but to actually palpate or press them gently, in order to get the true story.

There are some readers who do ink palm prints and read from that. I'm sure they get good results. I wonder though how they see the "false-positive" mounds using that method...

As we look at each mound, I'll be describing its position in the hand and referring to Figure 9, "Mounds" as a visual reference. It's important to know that these positions as described are approximate. A large mound may spill over into the space next to its traditional position, crowding its neighbor. When in doubt, it's a good idea to locate the mounds by looking at their positions in regards to the other mounds.

To put this in another way, when looking at mounds, the first mound is "Jupiter"; the second mound (often a dip or divot) is "Saturn"; the third is "Apollo"; and the mound on the pinkie edge is "Mercury" (looking at the finger edge of the palm and starting on the thumb side). This is the basic layout, regardless of whether they bulge out of their traditional placements or not.

Mounds are named after classical gods and goddesses. The nature of the deity that the mound is named for reflects the nature of the characteristic, or characteristics that mound represents. This is helpful for remembering what mound stands for what quality.

It's important to note that, as we review the mounds, I'll be describing different variations of each mound. As I do, I will be describing the most extreme versions of each variation, in order to give you the clearest understanding possible.

But your results may vary.....

Since the variations of any particular mound can be seen to a greater or lesser extent; the personality type of your querant will vary commensurate with the degree of variation of the mound.

As one example, for the mound of Venus which deals with sensuality and aesthetics, it's possible to be extremely sensual, or a little bit conservative on beauty, without being a Puritan.

In comparing the mounds in the dominant and non- dominant hands, you'll be looking at what "was" as opposed to what "is"; or what were the original tendencies and talents vs. what you're doing with them.

For example:

A person who formerly had poor self-esteem, but who has learned to believe in herself.

A person with natural artistic talent who isn't currently using it.

A person who was afraid to speak her mind, but has finally found her voice.

A hedonist who has learned to value substance over style.

A former doormat who has learned how to say "No".

An adrenalin junkie who has slowed down a bit.

We'll get into this in more detail as we visit each of the individual mounds....

Chapter Thirty-Five

The Mound of Venus -
Love and Beauty

Now that we've gone over the general aspects of reading the mounds, it's time to look at our first specific mound.

As a visual reference to mound location, please get out Figure 9, "Mounds". Place it where you can see it without touching or holding it, as both of your hands will be engaged with both of the hands being read (if you're practicing on another person).

Your hands should be cradling your querant's hands, with yours and the Querant's hands palms up and as level as possible (according to the tolerance of your querant for having her hands turned palms up). Your thumbs are on top over the querant's palms, and will rest on each mound as you read it, palpating to determine actual size and muscle tone of the mound.

The mound marked "A" is the mound of Venus.

Use your thumb to gently palpate or massage the mound of Venus.

Is it large and firm?

Is it very large, like an over-stuffed pillow?

Is it lean but muscular?

Does it look large but collapse when you press on it?

What is your impression of this mound?

Venus is the Goddess of Love, Beauty, and Sex.

In the palm, the mound of Venus is that, and so much more. The mound of Venus stands for sensuality, sexuality, and the love of things that delight the senses.

Pink, fuzzy bedroom slippers...

Really good chocolate...

A live concert with your favorite musician.....

The smell of fresh baked cookies....
Recliner chairs with heat and massage...
Or whatever floats your boat.....

If the mound of Venus is large and meaty, the querant is a very sensuous person. She likes people, things and experiences that look good. sound good, smell good, taste good, feel good. She is willing to go to great lengths to bring such experiences into her life.

She has a highly developed sense of aesthetics. She's "artistic"- not in the creating of art, but rather in bringing it together, and surrounding herself with it. Rather than clay or paint, Life is the medium of the art she creates.

She will put a good deal of time and effort into building an environment that is almost a "setting", with her as the perfect "jewel" therein.

It's not enough for her to have a pencil - she must have a pretty pencil.

She often (but not always) has a highly developed sex-drive. If she does not, she usually feeds her senses through other activities.

Take a quick look at her head line. If it's long and deep, she loves beauty and sensuous things, but has the good sense not to let this love lead her into risky or dangerous behavior.

If it's short, light, or broken, however, her sensual tastes run the risk of putting her in harm's way. She'll go to the edge, and possibly beyond...

Look at her fate line, too. If there's plenty of money there, she has the resources she needs for beautiful things and experiences. If it's light or broken, she'll need to husband those limited resources well to make her world beautiful.

This is another area where a good head line can help. Good judgment also applies to choosing wisely what she spends her money on, and getting the maximum bang for the buck...

Sometimes, you don't need a five pound box of chocolates.

Sometimes, you just need the one <u>perfect</u> chocolate.....

While reading for her, you can praise her for her taste, and her feel for beauty. You can caution her, if needed, to use good judgment when feeding her senses.

You can allude to her sensual nature, but should also be cautious about how much you discuss her sensuality. (Most venues are family oriented, and PG rated. Even for adult venues, there's such a thing as too personal.....) On this particular subject, less can be more.

If the mound of Venus is muscular, but lean and less mountainous, or more flat, the querant cares more that things do the job and work properly, rather than if they are beautiful or striking. She values function over form, and is not distracted by superficial external impressions from the true value within a person, thing or experience.

She won't necessarily say "No" to a nice piece of chocolate, but she will not build her life around the pursuit of chocolate (as her sister above might).

If she can get both effectiveness in function, and beauty in appearance, she'll be glad to take it. If she has to chose, she'll choose function every time.

When reading for her, praise her perceptiveness in seeing past the masks society wears. Remind her that it's a workable choice to have things that do the job <u>and</u> make her soul sing...

If the mound is flabby and flat, this querant has little interest in the joys her senses could bring her. She may even be a little repressed or numb; or have lost her body image somehow.

This can sometimes (but not always) be due to some kind of traumatic event.

When reading for this querant, it'd be a good idea to gently encourage her to do something to wake her senses up a bit. Maybe buy herself a bouquet of her favorite flowers, and enjoy the scent. Or engage in some physical exercise, such as dancing, or swimming.

Anything to re-establish her contact with joy....

Remember to examine the contrast of the mounds in both hands. What does this contrast tell you?

Is this a previously withdrawn girl who's living a Cinderella story, and finally blossoming?

Is this a former hedonist who's leaving the wild days behind, in favor of things of lasting value as opposed to superficial appeal?

The difference in this mound in the non-dominant and dominant hands can tell you this....

When it comes to the markings we've been looking at since early in this book, I don't often see them on the mound of Venus. You can look, of course, for a triangle for aesthetic gifts, or an "X" for conflicts regarding sex, and so on.....

The markings I see most on the mound of Venus are unique to this mound. If you see someone with a series of lines fanning out horizontally and diagonally across the mound of Venus, these are said to indicate people who support her, and are pulling for her success.

Go ahead, take a look now....

Where these are concerned, the more the merrier......

This concludes our basic tour of the Mound of Venus. On to the next mound!....

Chapter Thirty-Six

The Mound of Jupiter - Power and Leadership

On to the next mound! Next we'll be touring the mound of Jupiter, "B" on Figure 9, "Mounds". Please position your handout where you can refer to it while holding the hands of your querant.

Use your thumb to gently palpate or massage the mound of Jupiter.

Is it raised and muscular?

Is it enormous, out of proportion with other mounds?

Is it an angry red?

Is it flat, and flabby?

Does it look big, but collapse when you push on it?

What is your impression of this mound?

Jupiter is the king and the leader of the gods. He has power, majesty and strength.

The mound of Jupiter stands for leadership ability, self-esteem, personal power, motivation and independence. This is a mound that is going places (when it's developed properly).

If the mound of Jupiter is well-developed and muscular, this is a person with healthy good self-esteem. While he enjoys praise, he does not rely on external validation to feel good about himself. He gets his feelings of worth from living up to his own internal values.

He's his own best friend.

He has a realistic view of his talents, skills and abilities, as well as of the areas he could use some more work. He is appropriately proud of his achievements, without being egotistical or self-centered. He's an appropriate blend of proud and humble. He will toot his own horn, but only if he's really accomplished something meaningful and real. This self-recognition will be less about gathering praise or false self-esteem through external validation, and more about sharing the joys of achievement, and the results of his labor with others.

Internally motivated., he doesn't need someone else to pick his goals for him, or kick him in the tush to get him started. He chooses a goal, and goes for it, powered by his own desires and choices.

He sails guided by his own North Star.....

He's a natural leader. He easily brings people together, and motivates them to take action towards a common goal.

He may not choose to lead, but people will follow him anyway, because he looks like he knows what he's doing.....

When reading for this querant, you can praise him for his good self-esteem, and self-motivation. You can reinforce that it's not egotistical to take credit for things you've actually accomplished

You can also acknowledge his leadership skills.

Many querants of this type are ruefully a bit embarrassed that people follow them, even when they're not trying to lead. Let him know that many people would like to have their lives together in the way he already has, and that following him can be a way for them to be more together as well.

If the mound of Jupiter looks overly large compared to the rest of the hand (almost swollen) and especially if far "redder" than the other mounds, this querant may have some problems with ego.

He may even be an ego-maniac.

He likes things his own way, even if there's a better way, or if other people have different preferences.

He may demand shows of respect that are excessive, rather than chose to earn appropriate respect. He needs external validation.

He thinks he's super, and thinks other people should, too.

He's very motivated to get what he wants, and may even be ruthless in its pursuit.

He wants to lead, even when no one wants to be lead. He may be good at leading, but his self-centeredness can make him unpleasant to even be around, let alone to follow.

In reading for this querant, you'll need to choose your words carefully, in order for him to hear you. Explaining that it takes a strong man to make room in his life for the concerns of others may be helpful. It's also good to ask (gently) why he needs the accolades of others to feel good about his own life....

I rarely (thank heavens!) see this type of palm. Possibly, this kind of querant doesn't feel the need of input from a psychic...

If the mound of Jupiter is flabby or flat, this is a person with self-esteem problems.

This querant doesn't believe in himself.

He often second guesses himself, or calls himself names. (Ex: "I'm so clumsy!", "There I go, doing something stupid again!", etc.) He plays "If only" a lot ("If only I'd said that!", "If only I'd asked her out!", etc). A lot of this negative self-talk comes from things he learned in childhood, but, by repeating these things over and over (both out loud, and in his head), he perpetuates the self-abuse, and grinds his self image into the dirt....

He undervalues the things he can do, ("Shucks, that's nothing....") and the things that he's accomplished. He's quick to point out something else he hasn't done instead, and, since there is always something left undone, there's always a reason to feel like a failure.

His resulting view of himself as less than competent, and his fear of failing can often immobilize him, keeping him from trying to accomplish anything. He can therefore be living a half-life......

He fights change because he's afraid of failing. He needs external motivation to act.

He needs external validation to feel good about himself.... or safe at all. Because external validation feels good but fades quickly, he's vulnerable to living his life based on what others pressure him to do, rather than by what he himself values.

He's afraid to lead.

He's afraid to stand out.

I see a lot of folks with this kind of mound of Jupiter getting readings.

When reading for this person, be gentle but firm. Touch a bit on the positive aspects of this person. (We all have them.) Say you don't understand why this querant doesn't give himself credit for his stronger, more positive aspects. I find it's often handy to say that, if your querant had a friend in the same situation, he'd be giving that friend credit for his strengths. (Many folks like this have clearer sight when seeing their pluses in another, than they do in seeing them in themselves). Remind him that it's not egotistical to acknowledge the things that he has accomplished.

Encourage this querant to take the first step to be his own best friend (like the guy with the positive mound of Jupiter is).....

To believe in himself.....

Give him the encouragement he needs to shine.....

If the mound of Jupiter looks large, but collapses when you press on it, this person has self-esteem problems that he camouflages with a false display of confidence (or even arrogance!).

He believes that no one would love, or respect him if they knew who he really was, so he pretends to be something he thinks will be more desirable.

He sails under false colors, constantly afraid that he'll be found out, and that everyone will know that he's not what he appears to be.

When reading for this querant, it's important to (gently) explain how one can only be truly happy when one is being ones' self. That you can only be first rate at being yourself, and can only be second class at trying to be someone else.

That you need to be yourself, because everyone else is taken...

Tell this querant that there are people in the world who would love and respect him for who he truly is, and that those folks will never get a chance to if he won't let them in.

If he has a good head line, he has the good judgment to figure out who these people are. You should remind him of that as well.

Those are the people whose good opinion matters, not that of folks who are only happy if you'll be someone other than who you really are.

This querant will also need a lot of the support the person with poor self-esteem did, once you can coax him into considering coming out of hiding....

Since you've been working with applying the marks to various landmarks of the palm throughout this course, I'm sure you can already see how they'd apply to the mound of Jupiter, so I'm just going to give you some examples to get you started.

A cross on this mound could be a challenge to your leadership or a competitor.

A triangle could be special gifts in the area of self-esteem.

A square could be outside protection to your personal power and control over your circumstances (such as someone who's got your back, whether on this side of the veil or the other...).

A grid could be blockages to taking action and moving forwards.

And so forth....

What markings do you see on this mound?

What do they mean to you?

This gives you some working knowledge of variations of the mound of Jupiter that you might encounter.

Next stop, the mound of Saturn, where all sorts of interesting bits and pieces are found.....

Hand Notes

One question I frequently get asked is whether scars matter in a palm reading.

Yes, and no…

You don't read the scars when you read a palm.

However, if the scars cause the lines to shift, you read the lines as they finally lie. And if the injury causing the scar affects the structure of the hand (ex: damaging the mounds or losing a finger or part of the palm), this affects the reading as well.

Chapter Thirty-Seven

The Mound of Saturn -
Responsibility and Balance

Now it's time for the mound of Saturn. This mound is marked "C" on Figure 9, "Mounds". Once again, please position the handout where you can refer to it while holding both hands of your querant.

Use your thumb to gently palpate, or massage the mound of Saturn.

Is it soft and flabby?

Is it raised and muscular?

Is it a little depression with a muscular ring around the edge?

What is your impression of this mound?

Saturn is the Lord of the Underworld. He has dominion and power over Death and other hidden mysteries. He is responsible for the separation between the world of the living and that of the dead.

The mound of Saturn stands for reliability, responsibility, and respectability (and, in extreme cases, boringness and pocket protectors....). It also stands for depression and the Occult.

At first, this may seem an odd assortment, but as you work with it, it all comes together.

The mound of Saturn differs significantly in structure from other mounds.

In most mounds, the bigger the mound is (within reason), the more of that characteristic you have, and the better off you are for the most part.

Saturn is different.

With Saturn, there are three different types of mounds, each with variations of degree.

There is the raised mound.

There is the soft or flabby depression.

There is the little "divot" surrounded by a muscular ring in the mound of Saturn position.

These are the three options you'll be looking for as you read this mound.

It's also important to note that, if you have a recessed (or "divot") mound of Saturn, with well-developed or over developed mounds on either side of it, the oversized mounds may bulge into the space under the middle finger that belongs to Saturn. At that point, it's easiest to remember that the positions of the mounds are approximate, and that they can be located by their positions in relationship to each other and to the fingers (keeping in mind that Saturn may be a hollow as opposed to a bump...).

If the mound of Saturn is raised and plump or muscular, this is a person who is <u>overly</u> responsible.

This person has too much to do on her "To Do" list.

She probably does not delegate well.

This person was born with her hand up, saying "I volunteer!"

This is the person who takes care of everybody's cats while they're on vacation, and thereby never gets a vacation herself.

Now, being a giving, responsible person is a good thing, but this person takes it too far to extremes.

She lacks balance in her life.

This person is often so busy taking care of others that she forgets to take care of herself.

She is so busy nurturing the dreams of others around her that her own dreams wither on the vine.

She is at high risk of burn-out.

She doesn't know how to say "No!"

And she needs to learn.....

When reading for this person, it's important to emphasize

balance. Honor her for the good things she does, but remind her that she needs to take care of herself too, because this is the way to keep from burning out.

Give her feedback on things she can do (for example: delegate, set "good-enough" standards, schedule time for herself, etc.,) to start to bring more balance into her life.

In her case, the truth is that she may have been sacrificing herself for others for so long that she may have no idea how to nurture herself. She may need suggestions on how to start.

This person's first impulse tends to be to sacrifice herself for others. Because of this, it's often helpful to emphasize that, if she continues to martyr herself, she's likely to burn out and be unable to help anyone. If, she gives some of her time/energy/love to herself on the other hand, it will make her stronger, more balanced <u>and</u> more able to help others.

This makes finding balance between the needs of others and her own needs a "Win – Win" for the caring person, and something she's therefore more likely to do.

This type of Saturn is particularly common in the round (people - person) palm. When reading a palm, if you see a round palm, you should immediately check for the raised mound of Saturn. If the querant has one, this means she has no boundaries, and is prone to letting people walk all over her or take advantage of her.

Emphasize the need to be able to say "No!"

"No, you cannot wipe your feet on me."

"Thank you for thinking of me, but no."

"I'd love to, but I've already got too much on my plate."

"I know you're having troubles, but what you want, I'm not able to give. I can give you this much, and no more."

I like to make these folks a gift of a mantra I've been working with for awhile. I tell them that "I can do anything I want. I just can't do everything I want..."

This usually hits home. They'll laugh, but you can see the light bulb go off....

You'll need fast talking, pretty stories and good persuasion to open these folks up to the idea that their needs are as important as those of the people around them. Jokes, stories and vivid mental images work well for them (One image I like is talking about juggling chainsaws...)

The over-developed mound of Saturn is also commonly teamed with the head line slanting downwards (indicating imminent or present depression). These are the folks that have sacrificed themselves to the brink of burn-out. It's particularly important for folks with this variation of the head line and this kind of mound of Saturn to start nurturing themselves.

Any querants with overdeveloped mounds of Saturn need to be reminded to treat themselves at least as nicely as they do other people.

To treat themselves as the unique, beautiful, special children of the Universe that they are...

If you tell them that they're special and deserve to be treated with respect, many of them will weep. Be prepared for this. Have Kleenex. Make soothing sounds. There may be tears, but they're usually happy tears of release, and enlightenment.

If the mound of Saturn is flabby, collapses when you press on it, or is not present, this person is not someone you can count on.

She may "mean well", but it's really hit or miss whether she'll keep her commitments or not.

At a potluck, don't count on her to bring the crucial entree. Assign her a salad, or dessert, where (if she forgets) it's less of a problem.

It's not necessarily that she doesn't care, but rather about issues like lack of organization, lack of carry-through, distractibility, or lack of focus. She has a real hard time getting things together.

It can be a case where she honestly doesn't see that a promise means anything. She may see keeping her word as something unimportant, and expect people to forgive her failings indefinitely.

This doesn't mean she's a bad person, but may mean she's never learned how broken promises can destroy peoples' trust, and truly hurt them. She may not understand that promises broken can destroy trust, which is the bedrock of every human relationship

She may be decorative, as opposed to functional.

It can also be (sometimes) a case where she really is self-centered; and puts her own desires and tastes above anyone else's needs.

It's best to give her the benefit of the doubt though, if there are no other indicators in this direction.

When reading for this person, it's good to emphasize the importance of focus and keeping one's commitments. Talk about how trust, which is the foundation of all human relationships, will stand or fall based on how we keep the promises between us.

Show her how keeping her word will make her world better.

If the mound of Saturn is a round, little "divot" or depression surrounded by a muscular ring, this is the best of all options in this mound. A mound like this resembles the little rings to set your ball in that you see at a miniature golf course.

The person with this kind of mound of Saturn has the best balance of responsibility to herself and to others.

She knows how to help people without them taking advantage of her.

She knows how to say "No!"

She has good boundaries.

She treats herself as specially as she does other people.

She gives her time/her love/her energy to her own dreams, as well as the dreams of others.

Because she has this balance, she is unlikely to burn out, and will therefore be helping others, nurturing herself, and making the

World a beautiful place for a long time to come.

It is worthy of note that balance, as indicated here, is not a static "Pie-chart" with 1/3 for self, 1/3 for others, and 1/3 for the world. The kind of balance we're talking about here is an active, ever-changing process, dependant on the tenor of the moment.

The best illustration I can think of would be if you ever stood in the middle of a teeter-totter when you were a child. Your feet were rarely perfectly 50-50, but the balance averaged out in a fluid, living pattern.

When you read for this person, praise her for her balance, and remind her that it's not as common as she might think. Let her know that balancing the needs of others with her own will keep her alive and free of burnout.

It's particularly good to compare the palms for this mound.

If the non-dominant is flabby, and the dominant is a muscular divot, this is a person who let people wipe their feet on her in the past but is now learning to have good boundaries.

If it's the other way around, this person normally has good boundaries, but her boundaries are getting floppy (frequently because of crisis or busyness).

There are various other combinations you can work out by contrasting the non-dominant hand with the dominant one. In other words, contrasting what "was" or "could-have-been" with what "is"....

By now, you're an old hand at applying the markings to individual landmarks, so let's just look at a few examples.

A grid on the mound of Saturn would indicate obstacles that interfere with your keeping your commitments.

A cross would indicate conflict in regards to your responsibilities.

A square would indicate protection and support enabling you to follow through on the promises you've made.

A star would indicate an unusual occurrence connected with the promises you've made.

And so forth....

What would the markings on this mound say to you?

The mound of Saturn is said to also apply to depression, and the Occult. You can surely find this here, but I tend to look for depression on the head line (as previously described), and the Occult on the mound of the Moon and other psychic signs (yet to come).

Well, this gives you an overview of the wonderful, unique mound of Saturn.

Next stop, the mound of Apollo!

<u>Hand Notes</u>

Can you read for children? I've heard a lot of readers say that the futures of children are so undefined that they cannot be read reliably.

I have not found that to be the case, myself.

Some children do have only a few lines with more to develop later on. These kids are in the process of learning, growing and gradually choosing their paths.

Other children, however, have well-defined lines that look like they were put in with a blow torch.

Some children have many paths to choose from. Some arrive here with agendas and destinies.

And even destiny's children have free will, and the ability to change their futures.

I find that any child who is willing to be read can be read.

Chapter Thirty-Eight

The Mound of Apollo -
Arts and Sciences

We travel next to the mound of Apollo. This mound is marked "D" on Figure 9, "Mounds".

Use your thumb to gently palpate or massage the mound of Apollo.

Is it raised and muscular?

Is it raised and plump, but not muscular?

Is it flat and flabby?

What is your impression of this mound?

Apollo is the God of the Sun. He is often pictured playing the lyre and indeed gave the lyre to humanity.

The mound of Apollo deals with all things concerned with the Arts and or Sciences.

If the mound of Apollo is raised and plump but not muscular, the querant has a talent in an art or science that he is using partially. He may pursue it as a hobby, or in a dabbling or half-hearted fashion.

There's nothing wrong with making a gift in arts or sciences only one factor in your life. It's just worth noting that for this person, it's significant but not the primary focus.

If the mound of Apollo is raised and muscular, this person has a gift in an Arts or Science that is a Hunger or a Calling. This person probably builds their life around that gift. He is constantly practicing a sport, or studying botany, or trying out new water color painting effects. When you think of this person, you think of his talent, because it defines him and he defines it.

How much he will achieve with this talent depends not only

on the talent itself, but also on other factors such as persistence (thumb chain), motivation (mound of Jupiter), and balance between his needs and those of others (mound of Saturn). You can check these areas to find out what he may need to work on to make his calling a reality.

If the mound of Apollo is flabby or flat, the querant currently has no ability in an Art or Science.

Check the non-dominant hand. If there's signs of talent here, but none in the dominant, that usually indicates a talent that the person is currently not pursuing, or practicing.

If both are flat or flabby, arts and sciences are just not this person's thing.....

If the non-dominant hand indicates a talent that is not active in the dominant hand, the most frequent cause of that is a person that's so busy doing everything else and taking care of everyone, that he has no time for his own calling.

To check this, proceed immediately to the mound of Saturn. Is it the raised, muscular mound that indicates the over-committed, over-extended person? There's your key.

You need to talk to this person about bringing balance into his life, so that he can pursue his own gifts and talents. He may understand this better if you remind him that his talents can be as significant a gift to the world as the tasks he is currently taking on.

You may also want to talk to him about ways that he can find time for his talent in his busy schedule. One example would be to find a place in his home where he can have his painting gear set up and ready to go for 10-15 minute painting breaks. Another way would be to plan daily or weekly times when there is a special, self-directed activity for children, so Daddy does his thing and the children do theirs.

The number two reason for potential but no practice is lack of focus (no thumb chain). Talk to this person about ways to carry through, and actually practice the talent that calls to him.

You may sometimes find that when you talk to a person about a gift in the arts or sciences, that this person has no idea what you're talking about. Our culture isn't set up to support people in thinking about the arts and sciences as something that many of us actually do,

After all, only "special" people are stars in the arts and sciences. Right?

Wrong. But for many folks, the arts and sciences are terms so exotic that they seem beyond their reach.

You can help this person by naming different arts and sciences. Botany. Performance art. Inventing. Exploration. Handicrafts. Cooking.

You name it.

Another way to help someone like this is to ask them what's "juicy" for them. What do they r-e-a-l-l-y like to do? There's usually a clue in there.

Sometimes, you'll get someone who's been so crushed by life that they're just surviving. This person may have no clue what they enjoy, because their life is such a struggle.

For this person, try asking them what they really liked to do as a child. You can find the clue there.

For all of these situations, watch your querant. You'll know you've hit pay dirt when they straighten up, start to smile or even laugh. When suddenly, the Light comes flooding out of them.

Some folks won't even get their answer with these questions. Some people need to do the work, and find their secret talent themselves. For some folks, it's enough to know that there is a hidden talent. They can keep their eyes out for it themselves now that they know it's there.

If you can get specific, good. If you can't, it may be something the querant needs to discover for himself.

Do what you can, and move on.

Now, let's look at a few examples of marks on the mound of Apollo.

A triangle indicates an extra special gift in an art or science.

A star or asterix indicates an unusual, fortuitous occurrence. Possibly winning a competition, or creating a new innovation in the area of your talent.

Grids mean obstacles to overcome to get there.

A cross means conflict or competition (not of the nice type).

And so on.....

One of the questions that often comes up in palm readings is "What career should I go into?"

As you know, the first place to look at jobs is the fate line. You can find things like creativity, family influence, and career changes there.

The mound of Apollo is good for looking for special talents, as applied to work.

Other places to look include the head line (judgment, creativity, smarts, planning), heart line (emotional aspects), thumb (flexibility, persistence), mound of Jupiter (motivation, independence, leadership), and the mound of Mercury (which we'll be visiting in the next chapter).

This concludes our tour of the major sights of the mound of Apollo.

On to the mound of Mercury....

Chapter Thirty-Nine

The Mound of Mercury - Business and Communications

Welcome to the mound of Mercury. This mound is marked "E" on Figure 9, "Mounds". See it?

Use your thumb to gently palpate or massage the mound of Apollo.

Is it raised, and muscular?

Is it prominent?

Is it flat or flabby?

Is there a series of little vertical lines on it?

What is your impression of this mound?

Mercury is the messenger of the gods. He's swift as thought, and always on the go. He carries the caduceus, the winged staff with entwined serpents, which has become the symbol of the medical profession.

The mound of Mercury stands for business, and communications. It also has certain aspects that indicate the hands of a healer.

The mound of Mercury stands for communications and business.

These are rather different areas of life. There is a certain amount of overlap (many times, to be good in business, you need to be good at communicating with your customers) but there still can be points of difference here.

How can you tell which area is being referenced for a particular querant?

I find the best way to determine this is to trust my intuition. I place my thumbs on the mounds of Mercury, close my eyes for a minute, and "reach out" with my spirit for information on whether this querant is a master communicator, or the king of commerce, or both.

I then proceed from there.

Try it! You may be surprised with how much insight you get this way. (More information on this technique in chapter 50.)

If you're not totally comfortable with the intuitive technique yet, there are some physical characteristics that can support your impressions

If the fate line (which indicates luck, and money, remember?) is strong, this may be due to a good business head.

This is not an absolute indicator however, as you may have a great mound of Mercury, and a poor Fate line. This happens in someone for whom the money runs out as fast as it runs in. (Do you know someone like that? I know I do...). Check the heart line for forking, or feathering. If you see it, this may be the sign of an impulsive spender. Add in a severely sloping head line, and you may have someone that self-medicates by shopping.

If the mound of Apollo (Arts and Sciences) is prominent, as well as the mound of Mercury, you may have a great communicator, by way of singing, acting, or oration.

If the second mound of Mars (standing for emotional courage - yet to be covered in this book) is prominent, the querant may be a great speaker of Truths that defend people's rights, or change the world.

These landmarks are indicative though, as opposed to absolute. The best way to find whether this mound speaks to business, or communication is to trust your own intuition.....

If the mound of Mercury is muscular and raised, the querant has a talent in business and/or communication.

If the talent is in business, this person has a natural ability to make things run efficiently, effectively, and make money. Prosperity tends to follow him around like a little puppy.

Check his Fate line. If it's strong, he's affluent, successful, and should pay for the drinks.

If it's moderate, he's still a good businessman, but may have other additional business priorities (such as benefits to the community, or meaningful work) that may affect his financial intake. (He'll still be making as much as he wants. It'll just be that part of his pay is in other tender than cash). You can check for other landmarks, such as fate line (satisfactory amount of abundance or not based on the querant's priorities), pointed/conical fingers (Dreamer/Idealist), or mound of Saturn (serving one's own needs or those of others).

If his Fate line is poor, money either runs through his hands like water, or else he is good at making money for other people but not himself. (This last option tends to go with a poor mound of Jupiter. The person with low self-esteem may be good at making money, but feel unworthy to have it himself).

If his head line is strong, and more level, it further strengthens the efficiency and effectiveness of the business sense.

If the talent is in communications, this person has a natural ability to be able to get his message across. He has the gift of gab. He may talk a lot, or he may not. Either way, when he speaks, people will tend to listen because what he says makes perfect sense.

He doesn't just say words, but rather says the words that pass through the ears, and go straight to the heart, the spirit, the balls, or whatever else the communicator is aiming at.

He's really good at making that crucial connection.

He's also very persuasive. He can talk the back legs off a mule.

Now, I'm using speaking as an example, but this person's communication doesn't have to be by speech (whether classic oration, or simple one-on-one conversation). This type of person can connect with people by singing, or acting, or gesture, or any other manner of communication. He won't always excel in every mode (although some folks with large mounds of Mercury do), but will definitely have one or more communication techniques that he uses to excellent effect.

It's worth noting that he's not necessarily only promoting his own messages. Check the other features in his palm.

If his secondary mound of Mars (standing for emotional courage - to be discussed in a coming chapter) is well-developed, he'll probably be speaking out on behalf of the rights of others who are afraid to speak up for themselves.

If there is a mystic cross beneath the index finger (standing for the ability to lead or inspire others - to be discussed in the chapter on psychic signs), a well-developed mound of Mercury will strengthen his ability to inspire others to change their own lives, (hopefully for the better, although this is not necessarily guaranteed.).

If the mound of Mercury stands for both business <u>and</u> communications, this person can be the quintessential salesman.....

If the mound of Mercury is small but muscular, this person doesn't necessarily have the gift of gab, or the golden touch, however he has good, basic, functional skills.

He may not shine, but he'll get by.

If the mound of Mercury is flat or flabby, business and communications are not this person's strong suit.

In business, this person should be working in someone else's business, preferably for salary, doing familiar tasks. He won't be a brilliant innovator in business.

In communications, he'll probably either stumble over his words, or be the strong, silent type.

When looking at the mound of Mercury, it's a good idea to

compare the palms.

Is the mound small in the non-dominant hand, but large in the dominant one?

This tends to be a formerly shy person who's in the process of learning to speak his Truth. Check the lengths of both heart lines for supporting information (short/shy vs. longer/open).

This person needs encouragement to take appropriate risks in moving outside of his comfort zone, so he can be true to his beliefs and grow as a person.

Is the mound large in the non-dominant hand, but small in the dominant?

This person tends to be an extrovert who's currently in a position where he believes that it's not safe to speak his Truth. He's biting his tongue, because he knows that the Truth in his present situation may not only be unwelcome, but may actually hazardous to one degree or another.

The risk in this case may be a current one or a perceived risk left over from a previous traumatic experience (for instance, fearing that, if he opens up to the woman he's dating and lets her know how he really feels, that she may break up with him, leaving him alone.)

In this case, hazardous may be anything from risking ridicule or rejection, right up to actual physical harm.

Sometimes it's safer or wiser just to keep your mouth shut, but a prolonged period of denying your truth, or living in hazardous conditions can be unhealthy to body, mind, and spirit.

This person may need to have his situation acknowledged, and asked what option he'd chose in order to be true to himself once more.

One special type of marking that is specific to the mound of Mercury is the Medical Stigmata. These are little vertical lines on the mound of Mercury beneath the pinkie.

Medical stigmata tend to indicate the hands of a Healer. This can be mainstream medicine or alternative medicine, so they're equally likely on the hands of a Reiki master or an emergency room nurse.

They appear in the hands of someone who's either working, or would do well working in the area of healing, or related human-services helping field. When we speak of healing, this includes healing in body, mind, and spirit.

Some examples are:

        Doctor,
        Acupuncturist,
        Nurse,
        Energy healer, such as a Reiki practitioner,
        Therapist,
        Councilor,
        Herbalist,
        Chiropractor,
        Psychiatrist,
        Nutritionist,
        EMT,
        Macrobiotic chef,
        Certain types of police, or firemen,
        And so forth.

Not everyone who has medical stigmata will work in a healing field, but everyone who has them will have a natural talent for it. If he's not in such a field, it might be something worth considering.

While we're looking at markings, let's examine the influence of some of our more general markings on this mound.

A cross can indicate verbal confrontation - or, to put it another way, fights. It can also indicate business competition. (Remember to look at which arm of the cross is deeper to determine who's currently on top in this conflict.).

A grid can indicate widespread conflict in business or the

negative influence of nasty gossip on or about you.

A star can indicate a fortuitous event for your business.

A triangle can indicate a special gift for making your business hum.

A square can indicate the protection you need to speak your Truth.

What is your take on what the markings mean on this mound?

Please remember that, if you see horizontal lines on the mound of Mercury, they may be the ends of particularly long and significant marriage lines. If there are forks at the end of these lines, they are children lines. (Remember - this is one of the few points where forks are a good thing!)

This concludes the basics on what the mound of Mercury has to tell us.

Forwards, to the mound of the Moon (otherwise known as Luna)!

<u>Hand Notes</u>

What do you need to know about reading for children?

Well, children can benefit from many of the same things that an adult can in a reading, when adapted for age, attention span, maturity level and intellect.

Things you may have to adapt:
- Vocabulary (they may need simpler words);
- Age appropriateness (having someone "like you" vs. sensuality);
- Shorter attention span;
- Abstract concepts;

It's also good to ask the child what he'd like to know about, as he may not have the patience for a full reading (and there's some virtue in cutting right to the chase.)

Pay attention to his non-verbal communication - scowling or squirming will tell you that he needs different words or has heard as much as he can tolerate for now.

Any or all of these topics may or may not need adjustment, dependant on the individual capabilities of the child you're reading for. (Come to think of it though, I've used complex concepts with some children and had to use smaller words with some adults, so this is not always a function of age alone.)

If you pay attention to what your querant needs, children are fun and rewarding to read for.

Chapter Forty

The Mound of the Moon I -
Creativity and Intuition

Here we are at the mound of the Moon (also sometimes known as "Luna"). On Figure 9, "Mounds", this is the mound marked "F".

Use your thumb to gently palpate or massage the mound of the Moon.

Is it raised and muscular?

Does it look muscular but collapse when you press on it?

Is it flat or flabby?

What is your impression of this mound?

The other mounds are usually named for gods whose natures reflect the characteristics covered by the mound itself.

This mound is different. If it held true to the pattern followed by other mounds, I'd expect to see it called the mound of Diana, or Luna, for the Roman goddesses of the moon. I've occasionally seen the name Luna used for this mound by very old or obscure texts, however, for the most part, most references refer to this as the mound of the Moon.

The Moon is famed for energizing all things mysterious, magical, and non-material. People think of magic, whether for good or ill, as taking place in the light of the Moon. (For those of you who know that magic can take time at any time, and any place, yes, I know it can. These analogies tend to be drawn on the everyday beliefs of the general populace, as opposed to individual experience.)

The Moon creates inspiration, unusual concepts, thinking outside the box. Indeed, people whose thinking is eccentric enough to be thought of as unbalanced have also been referred to as "moon-struck" (or "luna-tics").

The mound of the Moon represents creativity and intuition.

Non-linear thinking, and problem solving by flashes of inspiration (rather than linear, logical problem solving) also tend to hang out here.

This is also one of the places that psychic abilities can be located.

Before we go into reading the mound itself, let's discuss the issues surrounding psychic phenomenon in the palm.

From my experience, there are two questions that are most likely to frighten someone you're reading for.

The first is "How long will I live?" This is understandable, as most people are more or less afraid of death, and few people (with the exception of some Goths) like to contemplate it in any detail.

The second question that is most likely to frighten a querant is "Am I psychic?"

Now I must admit, this makes no sense to me (probably because I accept the fact that I am psychic, and that most, if not all, other people are). The fact that a querant will sit with me indicates that he's not frightened per se of psychic ability itself, but many querants are frightened to find out whether they themselves have Talent (although it's o.k. with them if I do)....

I don't get it, but I don't have to. Experience tells me that this is seriously scary to many querants.

Now, a good reader will not blow off things they see, just because they'd be challenging, or uncomfortable to express. On the other hand, scaring a querant can many times cause him to shut down so he can't hear what you're saying, or benefit from what you have to tell him....

Your job is to "see", and to tell what you've seen in a way so that your querant can hear and benefit from it.

Sometimes this means being tactful, or choosing your words carefully.

Sometimes this means weighing the importance of this

knowledge for the querant vs. how challenging/scary it will be for him to have it.

I find that, for the most part, on the issues of life expectancy, and that of psychic skills, the best option is usually to ask the querant.

When you looked at the life line, you asked him "Do you want to know how long you'll live?" (This is not critical info unless his line is short, and he needs to make drastic changes to avoid an immediate demise. Free Will is still in action in such situations).

If he said "yes", you told him.

If he tensed up and said "no", you didn't, unless the risk was so imminent that he needed to take immediate precautions.

At that point, you talked about it being very important at the present point in his life to be especially concerned with taking good care of himself, and also taking extra care with safety precautions, such as driving carefully, and watching for hazardous conditions. An early death can come from illness or from accident or violence, so you're covering the bases indirectly. In this way, you've given him the information he needs without freezing him up so much that he can't use it.

Likewise, when looking at psychic ability, you check first to see if there's any ability in psychic areas. (If there's not, you don't want to offer to discuss things that he doesn't have much of. That's just teasing and cruel.)

If there are indications in this area, ask him "Can I speak to you about psychic things?"

The ones who are ready to hear will usually get bright-eyed and grin. Some querants are even eager or desperate, and are having experiences that leave them wondering if they're psychic or crazy. These folks will usually jump at the chance.

The ones who aren't ready, who're terrified at the concept, will usually startle, or freeze up. They'll tell you, "No".

You're not here to scare querants, or force information on them. If you tried to, the fear would make things so bad that they couldn't hear you anyway. Trying to force information on a querant in such a situation tends to be more about validating yourself as a reader than looking at the querant's needs or respecting his personal boundaries (what he's prepared for, and able to handle). It's like teaching someone to swim by tying him in a bag, and throwing him in the deep end of a lake.

In this case, shift to talking about creativity. You can also talk about "hunches". This is a safer term for him for the same. phenomenon, and can start him on the path to understanding this part of himself.

Empowering someone includes respecting his boundaries....

If the querant is open to the ideas of both creativity and intuition, how do you tell one from the other in this mound?

Well, first of all, creativity and intuition tend to be part of each other.

The highly creative person tends to get ideas through non-linear thinking, or intuitive "flashes".

The highly intuitive or psychic person tends to think about things in a highly original or creative fashion. (You tend to expect this from someone who sees magic and psychic perception as a normal part of life).

So, as long as your client is comfortable with both, they are both similar traits, and can be covered as a team.

If you find you have a need to differentiate, you can find supporting signs of creativity in the slant of the headline.

You can also find supporting signs of psychic ability in other psychic signs in the palm. (We will be exploring these in a future chapter after we've completed the mounds).

The most important indicator would be, however, what your own intuition tells you about this question.

If this mound is raised and muscular, this person has a goodly amount of creativity and intuition. He has instincts, hunches, "gut impressions". They're usually right on. If he lets himself listen to his "inner voice", it'll guide him well, and, the more he listens, the stronger it'll get.

Here's where things get a little complex.

Check his head line.

If his headline is slanted or creative, he probably doesn't have problems listening to his hunches, and following them. You can do him a service by cuing him in that this is actual psychic ability in action, so he can listen to himself more consistently, but he's probably already on that path.

If the headline is more level, it's another story though. The more level across the palm it is, the more logical, and a linear thinker he is. If he is this "logical" type (regardless of how much mound of the Moon there is, and how many other psychic signs there are), he will have a tendency to talk himself out of listening to his intuition.

He'll think "That's silly. How could I know that?"

He'll ignore the information when it could be useful.

And then, when he finds out he was right all the time, he could just kick himself.

Despite this, the next time he has a gut impression, he'll talk himself out of it again.

It's a vicious cycle - and the only time you won't see it with the combination of level/logical head line, and prominent mound of the Moon is when your querant has done the work to prove to himself in a concrete manner that his psychic impressions are for real.

If this hasn't happened, you can give him the information he needs to empower his psychic side to truly serve him.

Here's how...

Why do logic and intuition initially make poor teammates? It happens because logic and intuition speak two different languages. Intuition speaks the language of Faith. ("Believe it even though you can't see it.") Logic, on the other hand, speaks the language of Proof.

(I believe what I myself can touch or see.") The Faith of Intuition seems like nonsense to Logic.

To break out of this conflict, you need to have Intuition speak Logic's language so Logic can understand Intuition and have Faith in it.

When I see someone with the signs of logic and psychic together, I tell him he's really tuned in, and that he has feelings and hunches that are usually right on. I then tease him a little bit about how he talks himself out of them, and how it's really frustrating when he finds out again and again that his hunches were right. He usually laughs in a slightly abashed fashion, and agrees with me. I tell him it's because he is very logical (a good skill), but that logic and intuition don't always understand each other.

I then ask if he'd like a trick that would help get his logic and intuition working together.

If he says "yes", I advise him to get a little 3 x 5 notebook, something he can carry with him everywhere. Whenever he has a "hunch", I tell him to write three things in his notebook;

1) What his hunch was;

2) What he did about it;

3) And what would have happened if he followed his "hunch".

I tell him the truth: that within 6 - 9 months (for some people, sooner), he will have a notebook full of examples that show that, whenever he has a "hunch", he's usually right.

At some point during this, his logical mind will say "Oh, this is not silly....This is Science.....See, here is data!"

And suddenly, the brain will flip-flop and accept the psychic side of him as something genuine, real, and very useful. The brain and the intuition, which were formerly pulling in different directions and fighting with each other, will suddenly start pulling together as a team.

Just like a team of horses, when the Logic and the Intuition pull together, they can take you some wonderful places.

This process works for several reasons:

- Writing the intuitive hunches down encourages your querant to
  listen to his inner wisdom, rather than ignore it.
- Writing is a neutral activity, which doesn't trigger resistance or "talking self out of it" behavior.
- Developing concrete data that shows his psychic abilities are real puts the esoteric activity in a concrete form that the Logic can understand and accept.
- Listening more to the Intuition makes it stronger, so it creates more amazing situations that are not so easily explained away.
- And using a small notebook that is easy to carry makes the process easier so your querant is more likely to try it.....

A relatively simple process that can accomplish great things!

In regards to creativity, we've already discussed ways of speaking about that when we covered the head line. If you see a lot of creativity in this person's head line and mound of the Moon, it's good to reinforce that, as well as reference how this can strengthen other aspects of the hand. (For example: how great creativity can be useful in arranging a home to feed the sensuous nature of a prominent mound of Venus.).

There's more to the mound of the Moon, but we'll be seeing that in the next chapter.

Hand Notes

Having talked about reading for children, is it possible to read babies?

> Why, yes. The youngest one I've read was 6 weeks old. Important things to keep in mind:

- The baby is not impressed that you are some hot-shot psychic. You will have to **earn** every bit of knowledge you get.
- Once you start working with a baby, the clock is ticking. Make each moment count.
- You are reading to give info to parents, so they can meet their baby's needs.
- Please give them the free will lecture before you start. Once you start with the baby, you need to focus on entertaining him and efficient peeking at his palms.

> I like to work with the baby on mom's lap, in a stroller, or wherever he feels good. Showing delight with the baby helps, as does eye contact, silly voices and tickling, as tolerated. Watch the baby's non-verbal cues to let you know what he's tolerating vs. what scares him. And play with him, sneaking peeks at his palms and reporting to mom or dad as you go (I've found patty-cake and peek-a-boo both very effective, as is gentle tickling.)

> And enjoy him. He'll work with you more if you're both having fun...

Chapter Forty-One

The Mound of the Moon II -
More Creativity and Intuition

In our last chapter, we started our tour of the mound of the Moon (Mound "F" on Figure 9...) dealing with creativity and intuition. We looked at attributes covered by the mound in more detail; discussed querants' issues about psychic abilities and how to deal with them; looked at the skills and needs in a reading for someone with a strong mound of the Moon; and addressed how to deal with conflicts between a client's Logic and Intuition.

Whew!

But, wait! There's still more to be found in this wonderful mound!

Ready? Here we go, back to the mound of the Moon.....

Do you remember what your querant's mound of the Moon looks and feels like?

If not, go back and check it out now. Palpate or massage that mound gently.

What is your impression of this mound?

If this mound is flat or flabby, this person doesn't have much creativity and/or intuition.

He tends to act in a very concrete, linear fashion, and follow established patterns of behavior, either paths that have been made by folks who went before him, or routines that he has created for himself. (Warning - Ruts ahead.)

He doesn't trust his inner wisdom or gut impressions. This can cause a lot of trouble for him.

Check the shape of his palm. If it's square, he may by nature be very grounded and concrete. He may need extra evidence to show him that things he cannot see or touch are as real as more physical things. Give him proof, and he will accept his non-material skills.

Check his head line. If it's very level, he believes only in what he can see, touch, and prove. He won't understand or utilize anything that relies on faith, such as religion, philosophy, or differing belief patterns from his own. This can weaken him in times of crisis.

He won't understand, and may even be impatient with other people who base portions of their lives on faith or beliefs. This can be rough on relationships, whether they're romantic, family, friends, or any other human interactions.

Check his heart line. If it's short or light, he may be afraid of his instincts, and emotions. Afraid that he'll lose control if he goes out of the area of concrete knowledge and logic.

He may not only be afraid of his own instincts and emotions, but also of those of others.

Check his life line, and his fate line. Are there islands covering the time you're at in his life? He may be trapped in a dead-end job or an unhappy life path that's squeezed the ability to dream out of him.

Check his mound of Jupiter. If his self-esteem is poor, he may automatically discount any information or ideas that come from his inner wisdom as unworthy, deferring always to external validation.

Most of all, check both hands.....

There are many places in the palm where it's good to check both palms. The mound of the Moon is one of the better ones.

As you remember, the non-dominant hand gives us information on the potential you were born with, and the dominant hand tells us what you're currently doing with it. In the area of psychic ability, this can be very useful information, particularly because these skills can so frequently be confused with logic, drama, or wishful thinking.

I don't know if everyone is psychic (I haven't met everyone

yet...).

- My belief, based on observations and personal experience, is that psychic ability seems to be hard-wired into the human system;
- with certain possible exceptions, we're all psychic to one degree or another;
- and the amount of actual psychic ability we have is a combination of:

  ○ genetics. (Yes, certain types of abilities and amounts of abilities as well, tend to run in families),
  ○ things that happen to us throughout life,
  ○ and finally the amount of work that we put into developing and using it. (Psychic ability seems to be like a muscle. If you exercise it, it grows stronger…)

In keeping with those beliefs, I've seen people with little psychic ability, people who have great natural ability but deny it, people who've worked to develop beyond their own innate talents, and every other combination you can think of...

So let's look at both hands...

If both mounds of the Moon are flat or flabby, there's little to no intuitive or creative juices here (I've never seen such a situation, but theoretically it might exist).

If the mound of the Moon is large in the non-dominant hand, and smaller in the dominant, this person has a great deal of psychic power that he's not using. Check his head line - is it that he's talking himself out of it? If not, he may not be aware that he's psychic, or how psychic he is.

Cue him in. I find showing the client how to palpate his own mounds of the Moon is usually convincing. (Watch the light bulb go off...)

Now there's nothing wrong with not using a gift you have at any current moment. (Ever buy cleaning supplies in bulk? You don't usually use everything right away....) You've got your whole life to use your talents, and Free Will includes the right to <u>not</u> use a talent even if you have one....

It's just good to know you have that potential. People don't always realize the amount of innate psychic ability they have....

It's good for such situations to have a couple of good starter reference books in mind, since you don't have time to immediately teach clients everything about using their abilities.

If you're prepared, you can cue him in that he's psychic, give him basic information, and refer a starter book if he wishes to go further.

If the mound of the Moon is larger in the dominant hand, this person has taken his natural gifts, and worked hard enough that he has developed his actual abilities beyond the gifts that he was given.

This is to his credit, because everything he has attained beyond his gifts is something he has earned himself through his own dedicated labor, learning and effort. Give him a pat on the back - he deserves it.

It is worthy of note that a person can actively develop any talent, including psychic ability, beyond his natural abilities without being consciously aware he has a gift. This is particularly likely in the psychic field. He'll think of it as "instincts", "hunches", or that he just "had a feeling" about things.

You may talk to your querant about this, and find that he isn't aware that that's what he's doing. Be prepared with examples of the "coincidences" that indicate more awareness beyond the five senses than are logical. (My favorite is thinking about someone you haven't talked to for awhile, the phone rings, and it's your long-lost friend on the line...)

If both mounds are large and meaty, this is usually someone who's either actively using their intuitive gifts, or otherwise thinks that he's just the luckiest person alive, because his hunches are usually right on.

Be sure to compare both mounds. This gives you useful information on where your querant is, and where they need to go next...

Let's take a look at the effect of some markings on this mound....

If there is a triangle on this mound, there is an extra special gift of creativity or intuition (probably in a specific area.).

If there's a grid, this person's gift is probably out of control, and making life hard for him. (For instance, a person with telepathy who can't shut the thoughts of others out of his own head.)

If there's a square, there is protection for this person in the areas of creativity or intuition (ex: a guardian spirit actively intervening to protect him from harm.).

If there's a cross or "x"s, there's some kind of conflict centered on creativity or intuition (usually from an external source.).

A star here indicates an extraordinary event in this area (usually positive.).

Look for any markings on this mound. What do they say to you?

The mound of the Moon has much to tell us about our creativity and our intuition. In an upcoming chapter, we'll be looking at other landmarks that give us additional information and more specifics about our senses beyond the basic five.....

But first, the final mounds - a set of twins!

Meet you next chapter on the mounds of Mars.

Hand Notes

Legend has it that Aristotle discovered a treatise on the art of reading hands on an altar dedicated to the god Hermes. It is said that the work was in Arabic and written in letters of gold.

Aristotle is credited with writing some of the earliest surviving texts on palmistry, including "Chiromantia".

Chapter Forty-Two
The Mounds of Mars I
Physical Courage

Here we are at the final mounds-the mounds of Mars. As opposed to the other mounds, here there are two matched mounds, both falling under the aegis of Mars.

To locate these mounds, please consult Figure 9, "Mounds".

The first mound is marked "G1", and falls between the mound of Venus (at the base of the thumb), and the mound of Jupiter (at the base of the index finger.

The second mound is marked "G2", and falls between the mound of Mercury (at the base of the pinkie), and the mound of Venus (the heel of the hand on the pinkie side of the wrist)

Mars is the god of War. He is fearless, courageous and a true man (god) of action.

The mounds of Mars deal with courage, and the action we take based on that courage.

The first mound ("G1") deals with physical courage.

The second mound ("G2") deals with moral and emotional courage.

Let's start with the first mound of Mars ("G1"). This is the one that is located on the same side of the palm as the thumb. It deals with physical courage.

Use your thumb to gently palpate or massage this mound.

Is it raised and muscular?

Is it very prominent or large?

Is it muscular but lean or flat?

Is there little muscle or tone in this mound?

What is your impression of this mound?

If this mound is muscular and of a moderate size, this person has an appropriate amount of physical courage.

She enjoys excitement, and seeks out new and exciting experiences, but is not an adrenalin junkie.

She enjoys a good balance in her life between excitement and peace; and makes the most of whichever comes her way. If times are challenging or dangerous, she can handle it. If times are calm, she can roll with that, too.

She can cradle a baby, fight a forest fire, slay a dragon, bring home the bacon, and fry it up in a pan. (Not all at the same time, of course. Multi-tasking like that would show up on the mound of Saturn, remember?)...

This is a capable person, with a healthy, balanced attitude. She's the kind of person you want to be standing next to if you find yourself in the middle of a disaster movie (or better yet, the kind you'd want to be yourself...).

If this mound is muscular and large, this person is a thrill seeker.

She loves adrenalin, and can't get enough of it.

She may seek out and practice risky or dangerous activities.

Motorcycle stunt work. Running the bulls in Pamplona. Bungee jumping. Un-safe sex. Federal politics. These may be leisure activities, or be part of her job. (Indeed, she may choose a career based on the potential for excitement...).

She's in it for the thrill.

She needs that "rush" from excitement. If she doesn't have it, things don't seem natural or right. In such cases, she may do things just to "stir things up a little".

Crank calls. Shop-lifting. Playing two boyfriends against each other.

She's not a bad person. She just craves excitement, and sometimes that leads her to foolish places (Check her head line. A sensible headline can channel this into more excitement with less potential for trouble.) She's not necessarily looking for trouble, however, since she doesn't always think about the long-term effects of creating "excitement", Trouble often finds her...

I'll often grin at this person and say she's a "rascal", or (if it seems appropriate) a "troublemaker". (Use this word carefully. It's a delight to the right person, but "rascal" is usually a safer bet.)

She'll grin back or crack up (and if her friends are with her, they'll break into peals of laughter too). I tell her that she loves excitement, and that (if there's not enough excitement around) she'll "make things exciting". (For instance – "Look! There's a whole bunch of buttons! Let's push them all, and see what happens!...")

At this point she's pleased, because I'm acknowledging the delightful side of her (and this can be delightful, rather than stressful...). Now she can hear me when I add the statement that making things exciting sometimes gets her into terrible trouble, and that it's not always in her best interests to go there.

It's o.k. to like excitement. It's just a good idea to look before you leap.

This person needs to learn that sometimes it's o.k. for things to be boring (and that it can be preferable to have a dull experience than go into monstrous trouble because you can't tolerate calm....).

If the mound is muscular but lean, this person can face danger but has no need for it.

If given her choice, she'll prefer a peaceful, predictable, non-scary life, but if a plane crash, or severe family illness, or national invasion moves into her sphere of influence, she'll deal with it. She won't like facing such challenges, but somehow she'll manage.

And once the challenge ends, she'll go back to her peaceful

routine.

If this mound is flat or flabby, this person is cautious and avoids risk and danger (at least of the physical type.).

Once again, we need to compare both palms.

If the mound is small in the non-dominant hand, and larger in the dominant, this is a cautious person who is learning to expand her comfort zone, and do more adventurous things. Cheer her on.

If the mound is larger in the non-dominant hand, and smaller in the dominant, she had her wild and crazy youth, but has become more cautious as she's gotten older. Praise her for gaining better balance.

If both mounds are small, she's always been a peaceful, low-risk type of person.

If both mounds are large, once a thrill-seeker, always a thrill-seeker....

On to the effects of markings on this mound.......

A square on this mound can indicate a special degree of protection from harm while pushing the limits...

A cross or "x" here can indicate drama or excitement caused by interpersonal conflict (ex: those multiple boyfriends noted earlier in this chapter ...).

A star on this mound can announce a particularly exciting or dramatic event (most likely positive...).

A grid can indicate challenges or danger from all sides.

A triangle can indicate a gift for living on the edge without going over it.

What do these markings say to you when you see them on this mound?....

This concludes our tour of the first mound of Mars, reflecting physical courage.

Next stop-the second mound of Mars. It's all about emotional and moral courage.

The courage to stand up for what you believe in...

<u>Hand Notes</u>

In addition to Aristotle, some well-known practitioners of palmistry included Hippocrates, Galen, Julius Caesar and Alexander the Great.

Chapter Forty-Three

The Mounds of Mars II-
Emotional and Moral Courage

At last, we come to the final mound - the second mound of Mars. This mound is the mound labeled "G2" on Figure 9, "Mounds". It falls on the pinkie edge of the palm, between the mound of Mercury (at the base of the pinkie), and the mound of the Moon (the heel of the hand).

And so, on to the second mound of Mars....

Use your thumb to gently palpate or massage this mound.

Is it raised and muscular?

Does it look raised, but collapse when you press on it?

Is it flat or flabby?

What is your impression of this mound?

As noted in our previous chapter, Mars is the god of War; fearless, courageous, and a true man (god) of action.

Both mounds of Mars deal with courage, and the actions we take based on that courage.

The first mound of Mars ("G1") dealt with physical courage, the lack of it, and (in extreme cases) thrill-seeking.

The second mound of Mars ("G2"), which we'll be learning about now, deals with emotional and moral courage.....

It's the mound of walking our talk, of putting our money where our mouth is, of living with integrity. It's the mound of facing our fears, and overcoming them. It's the mound of heroes, and leaders, and people who change the world.

It's the mound of doing the right thing.

I'm a really big fan of this mound. If I had to choose one mound I wanted to be at its best, this is the one I'd chose....

If this mound is raised and muscular, this person is someone who does the right thing, even if she's alone, even if she faces opposition, even if it's dangerous or scary. She has values and she follows them, even when it makes her life harder.

She lives with integrity.

She follows her own path, and has little interest in following the crowd. If she pursues similar interests and pastimes to the people around her, it will be because she wants to do a particular thing, not because of peer pressure, or fitting in with everyone else. Because of this, she may stand apart from her fellows.

She has inner coherence in her life. What she does from day to day is in harmony with what she believes, and, because of this, she has relatively little to regret in her life. What little she does have to regret is mainly based around the actions of others (The damage folks do to their self-esteem by caving in to bullies. The financial crises they create by "keeping up with the Joneses". The ways folks compromise their spirits to try to impress others....).

She'll tend to follow the rules and laws of her situation, unless those rules or laws violate what she believes to be right. She doesn't break the rules without a good reason, and, if she feels laws are unjust, she's often the person that will launch or empower the movement to change these laws.

This may make her an uncomfortable person to live with, unless one has similar priorities or can respect them in others. She is not comfortable "going along" with things she thinks are wrong. She may do it for awhile to serve what she sees as a greater good (for example, a relationship with one she loves, or a movement she believes in) but eventually, the conflict between what she believes in and what she does will drain her, or even tear her apart.

To be healthy and whole, she needs to live with integrity.

To walk her talk...

If you love her, you'll need to be ready to support her doing the right thing, even if it makes life more complicated or uncomfortable.

The payback is that you can count on her to do right by you. Be honest. Keep her promises. Support your dreams.

The well-developed second mound of Mars is the sign of the paladin, the white knight, the person who's here to make this world better, whether in a quiet way or a bold one. She may or may not have an official cause, but her choice to live her values has a significant effect nonetheless.

She does the right thing - and because she does, not only is her life better, but the world around her is too........

This person needs to hear from you that it's a good and valuable thing for the world for her to do the right thing, even if she's not always appreciated for it. That she may need to be brave sometimes.

That what she does matters......

It's worthy of note that the concept of "doing what's right" may have considerable variability.

Some concepts are (more or less) universal:

To keep your word;

To treat other people as you would want to be treated;

To not oppress those who are weaker (such as children....);

To work and play nicely with other children (of any age...);

To do no murder;

And so forth...

Other beliefs are more individualistic....

So people with highly developed secondary mounds may have different, and indeed opposing, beliefs on what is the "right thing to do".

Some examples?...

- Republicans, and Democrats;
- "right-to-life", and "right-to-chose";
- Conservationists, and loggers;

- Liberals, and conservatives;

It can get pretty individualistic.

Just remember, a well-developed 2nd mound of the moon does not always mean a person you'll like or be comfortable with.

It just means you can count on her to live her beliefs consistently.

To be who she is....

If this mound looks large, but deflates when you touch it, this person puts on a show of living her values, but collapses under pressure.

She wants external validation, and is vulnerable to the opinions of others. Because no one is totally tuned in on what's best for every other person, she's likely to end up living someone else's dream, instead of her own; knowing it; and being very angry with herself for caving in to others.

In a reading, she needs your encouragement to be herself, rather than a poor imitation of someone else.

A couple of examples that I like:...

"Be yourself - everyone else is taken..."

"You can never be anything, but second rate at being anyone other than yourself. You can only be first class at being YOU...."

"If other folks don't like who you really are, to heck with them if they can't take a joke!...."

You get the idea......

If this mound is flabby or flat, this person fears confrontation, and will run a mile in tight shoes to avoid it.

She will go along with whatever seems safest, easiest, and least controversial. She is vulnerable to every little wind that blows from a validation standpoint.

She doesn't want to stand out, except possibly by fitting in in an extravagant way. It's o.k. to have an over-the-top hair-do, if it's the "in" hair-do that everyone wants. It's o.k. to be extravagantly wealthy, if everyone around you values that.

She is even more vulnerable to external validation or criticism, than her sister discussed previously. Because of this, she spends a lot of time living in fear.....

"What if I don't fit in?"....

"What if they don't like me?"....

"What if I do something that makes me look like a fool?"....

This vulnerability can make her do things that get her in trouble, just to win the approval of others. (Check her head line for good sense, which can help to compensate for this.) It can make her waste her life living the dreams of others, instead of being who she's here to be.

Even if she's not actively courting external validation, she usually has problems standing up for herself, or the rights of others who need her strength (such as her children).

This kind of mindset can also be attractive to abusive partners, or "friends" who like someone who co-operates with being bullied.

Making your self-esteem dependant on the variable opinions of others is a pretty miserable way to spend your life. Denying your personal truth over and over again is like the soul's "Death of a Thousand Cuts"....

Your client needs you to confirm her worth and value in the world;

She needs to hear that she has rights that matter;

She needs to be told that it's important to be who she really is, rather than who someone else thinks she should be;

That if she becomes authentic, her true friends will still stay with her. That if the phony friends drift away, who needs fake friends?;

That she needs to move outside her comfort zone, and stand up for herself and for the others who need her;

That courage and integrity are two of the most important factors of having a happy life;

A life where she can live with herself:

Because, at the end of the day, yourself is all you got....

Give her the strength she needs to get started.

Here's another place where it's good to compare the palms.

If the non-dominant second mound of Mars is prominent, and the dominant one not so, this is often a person with great inner strength who hasn't discovered it yet.

I like to say "You have an inner Amazon, who's sitting inside of you smoking cigarettes, reading magazines, and wondering "So, when are you going to get to me, eh?" You're stronger than you know." to this querant. She usually laughs and relaxes.

She's then ready to talk about moving beyond her comfort zones.

Talk to her about extending her horizons.

The large non-dominant second mound of Mars, and small dominant one can also be someone who's been through a great deal of trauma or challenge that's caused her to hide her light under a bushel.

Check her heart lines - is the non-dominant long (open) and the dominant short (afraid to trust)?

Check her mounds of Jupiter - is the non-dominant good-sized (good self-esteem) and the dominant deflated (damaged self-esteem)?

Check her mound of Mercury -is the non-dominant large (good communication) and the dominant flat (keeping her mouth shut)?

These are all signs of the wounded warrior who may have experienced so much pain that the life has been crushed out of her.

She needs you to remind her of who she really is, and that, while we sometimes pay a price for living with integrity, it's still important to do.

Give her what she needs to help her relight the fire within.....

If the non-dominant second mound of Mars is small and the dominant large, this person has overcome her fears to become her authentic self.

This wasn't easy. Give her kudos for doing so, and for doing the right thing.

If both mounds are well-developed, this person is the real deal. She has always been a person of integrity.

Congratulate her on that.

If both mounds are small, this person has always been afraid of controversy or confrontation.

Gently ask her if she's happy with her life. If not, it may be time to start to face those fears.....

Go easy with her - it's hard for her to break free.

By now, you should be experienced enough to figure out yourself what the marks mean on this mound, but here are a few examples:

A square means protection in overcoming ethical challenges;

A cross means conflict with someone with different values;

A star means an amazing experience while doing the right thing;

A grid means ethical challenges coming from all sides;

And so forth....

What do these marks mean to you on this mound?

This concludes our tour of the final mound of the palm, the second mound of Mars. In our next chapter we'll go into an area of specialization that is frequently of interest to querants - the signs of psychic ability (both active and latent).

Figure 10 – Psychic Signs

A – Mound of the Moon
B – Line of Intuition
C – Mystic Crosses
    C1 – The Artist;
    C2 – The Student;
    C3 – The Leader;
D – The Girdle of Venus
E – The Ring of Solomon

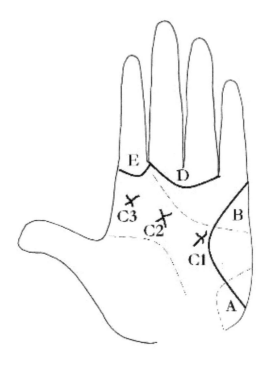

Figure 10 – Psychic Signs

Chapter Forty-Four

Psychic Signs I

We've learned the lines.

We've learned the mounds.

We've looked at hand shapes, and finger shapes, and many other landmarks, such as marriage lines and bracelets.

We've discussed ethics, Free Will, handedness, and much more.

We've looked at ways to address the specific topics of health, romance, and career.

Now it's time to look at another important topic.

The topic of psychic ability.....

I don't know if everyone is psychic....

I haven't met everyone yet....

It is my experience, however, that most (and possibly all) of us have at least latent psychic tendencies.

In my mind, the amount of ability seems to depend primarily on what your family passed on to you (there does seem to be some psychic strengths and tendencies which are genetic...), and on how much work you do to develop them (kind of like "pumping iron" with the spirit...).

Psychic ability seems to be hard-wired into our genes as part of being human.

Even if you aren't aware that you have such talents; even if you don't study, or practice in order to get better at them; you'll probably find a string of little "co-incidences" that are really your psychic talents peeping through the facade of everyday physical life.

You know the kind of thing -

When you think of someone you haven't seen in a long time, the phone rings, and it's that person;

When you start humming, turn on the radio, and hear the same tune;

When you know you can't trust someone, but can't put your finger on why;

When a mother has a sudden urgent need to pray for her child, and later finds out the child was in extreme danger at that exact moment;

There are many examples happening around us every day.

Unfortunately, society tends to view such things as coincidence, fantasy, or any other pretty phrase for something that it doesn't want to admit exists.

This means, if someone has psychic abilities, you may not only be doing a reading for her.

You may be the most accessible (and possibly only) resource she has on what is truly happening in her life, and how to either develop it or live with it (depending on what she's presently ready for).

So you need to be prepared to deal with this topic at whatever level the querant is at....

The question of psychic ability is an ambiguous issue for querants.

For many querants, it's a frightening issue, one of the two most frightening in the palm (for a more detailed discussion of this, please refer back to chapter 40, on the mound of the Moon).

Many people are perfectly fine with the idea that a reader is psychic, but find the idea that they themselves are psychic very spooky.

On the other hand, many querants are very curious about this. It's not the most frequent area asked about by people by any means; however, if you refer to it, many querants will suddenly "brighten up", grin, say "of course you can tell me about that ... ", or otherwise indicate extreme interest in the area.

For most folks, it's one extreme or the other.....

Because of this, when I get to this area of the palm, I look to see if there's anything significant indicated first.

If there's not much indicated, it's best not to discuss this area (because it's kind of a tease...).

If there are signs of significant psychic ability, I ask, "Do you mind if I speak to you about psychic stuff?...."

If my querant gulps, turns pale, averts her eyes, tenses up, says "I don't want to hear it...", or otherwise indicates fear, I skip over it.

Forcing information on someone who's scared to hear it is worse than useless (and possibly damaging) to her. It's important to respect a querant's need and right to get information in a way that she can hear and benefit from it. Knowledge to empower her, not freeze her with fright....

If she's not ready for that information, she won't benefit from it.

If you can't find a way to present it so she can hear it, now is not the time......

If, on the other hand, you start to get signs of interest such as noted above, feel free to proceed....

Sometimes you'll get both - signs of fear and signs of interest. These tend to be folks who are feeling the initial stirrings of ability, but find it so very far outside their personal experience and knowledge that they also are a bit spooked (metaphysical knowledge, experience, and training being rather irregularly distributed in this day and age...).

This person wants and needs your information; but you need to go gently, and chose your words carefully, in order to keep your information accessible to her.

Keep her comfortable and relaxed, and you can help her.

The client who's beginning to experience her own psychic abilities can certainly benefit from a well-done reading.

She may, however, need more than that....

For some clients at this level, the most beneficial thing you can give her is independent confirmation that psychic phenomenon are real. That she herself is psychic. That she's not lying to herself or going crazy.

Check her hands for signs of what kind of abilities and how much she has (potential/non-dominant and active/dominant). If the signs are there, you can give her useful feedback that may relieve her mind.

I've had many clients sit with me who thought they were crazy, paranoid, or living in a horror movie, when all that was happening was their own abilities were beginning to surface. Many times, I'll be reading for someone who accurately sees the truth of a situation, but has people telling her that she's wrong or delusional. This can be very destructive when she can feel they're lying or wrong, but ends up questioning herself.

Many times, the first signs come as very realistic, symbolic, or prophetic dreams. This is a classic phenomenon. It's because, when you sleep, your conscious mind is out cold but your unconscious is still aware.

The conscious mind includes judgment. This is a useful skill that keeps you from doing foolish or dangerous things. Judgment however also includes the part of you that says "Oh, that's silly. How could you know that?" when your psychic side is trying to tell you something.

The unconscious mind has most of the magick and psychic abilities, and no judgment whatsoever.

When your conscious mind sleeps, and isn't telling you that you aren't psychic, your unconscious lets your psychic side out to play, often through psychic dreams. (Not all dreams are psychic - but some are...).

Your client can get the reassurance she needs that these phenomenon are real, both by the accuracy in your reading, as well as the things you can tell her about her own abilities that help her put things together (many times such a reading becomes a series of major "A-ha"s !).

In addition to confirming her gifts, you should be prepared to give her some direction on how to follow up on her abilities, whether developing them or just plain living with them. She'll probably need more information than you can give her in one reading.

It's good to have the names and authors of a few good books to start out with for different areas. I've got one I recommend for general psychic skills, and a couple especially for empaths.

It's also good to know local resources you can send her to for additional training by ethical teachers. It's o.k. to recommend yourself as long as you give other options as well. (After all, since she's sitting with you, she may already feel comfortable with you. That's important for a teacher /student relationship.)

Finally, if the situation permits, it's good to be prepared to be able to do some very basic beginning training. I've stopped in the middle of a reading to explain how to start building basic energetic shields more times than I can count....

This querant may need a business card or contact information from you so she can follow-up with you on any additional questions that arise as she progresses.

Give her what she needs to start to get a handle on things.

An additional point that's worth knowing when you go into the area of psychic ability is that, like ice cream, psychic ability comes in all different flavors.

One psychic may have clairvoyance, and see visions.

Another may be clairaudient, and hear voices (real, but non-corporeal ones, as opposed to the voices of a guilty conscience, or a troubled mind...)

A third may be clair-sentient, and just "know" things outside of the sphere of her five senses.

A fourth, empathic, and really tuned into feelings, and other "vibes".

And there are many more options than this...

To make it even more fun, many of us have more than one ability, making for one big glorious mish-mash of talent, and input.

There are different lines and landmarks that can give an indication of where in these areas a person's particular talents lie. We'll be getting into that more as we make our way through this chapter and next one.

Like other landmarks reviewed before, the area of psychic ability is one where it's a good idea to check both palms.

If a psychic landmark is light/low/minimal in both hands, there's just a touch of the talent.

If it's dark or prominent in both, this person is actively using her talents. (Interestingly enough, you may see this pattern in the hands of someone who's not actively aware of her psychic ability but "trusts her instincts" fully. You don't have to call it psychic ability for it to function, and function well...)

If a psychic landmark is dark/deep/prominent/raised in the non-dominant hand, and lighter or lesser in the dominant hand, your querant has a good deal of psychic ability that she's not using at the current time.

She may be very surprised to hear that she is psychic.

If a landmark is prominent in the non-dominant hand, and minimal or non-existent in the dominant, your querant may not even know she has abilities, or even that there's a possibility that psychic phenomenon is for real.

She may even be in heavy denial about this.

Check her headline - is it very level? Is her palm square? She'll only believe in what she can see, and touch; and psychic things may seem like fantasy. This querant may need some kind of proof to accept her abilities as real.

Check her heart line - is it short? She may be afraid of her emotions, and find it difficult to trust her "instincts".

For more explanations on ways to address this, please refer back
to chapters 40 and 41. The techniques described there can also be applied to other psychic signs.

The landmark that is more defined in the non-dominant hand than the dominant one can also indicate some kind of traumatic event that has caused your querant to doubt or shut down abilities that she previously enjoyed.

Check for other signs of trauma, such as:

- a star recently on the life line;
- a change in the head line from "creative" to "logical";
- a shortening of the heart line, or increase in chaining or feathering, indicating emotional trauma or stress.

If these signs are present, they can support a reading of a traumatic blockage, or shut down.

If a psychic landmark is more evident in the dominant hand than the non-dominant, then your querant has taken the gifts she was given, and worked hard to develop beyond them.

Good for her! Praise her for taking her talents and running with them, as you would in any area where a client has worked hard to be

----

On to the metaphysical landmarks!

For visual reference, please look at Figure 10, "Psychic Signs". The five basic landmarks of psychic ability that I look for are listed here

The first is the mound of the Moon, which gives an overview of the presence, and amount of psychic ability and energy. For more details, refer to the chapters 40 and 41. This landmark is listed as point "A".

The other four major landmarks I look for are:

The Line of Intuition, listed as landmark "B";

The Mystic Crosses, listed as landmarks "C1", "C2", and "C3";

The Girdle of Venus, listed as landmark "D"; and

The Ring of Solomon, listed as landmark "E".

Feel free to take a moment to check your hands, and see how many of these landmarks you see there.

I'll wait....

The Line of Intuition (landmark "B") is a large loop on the pinkie side of the palm. Both ends tend to either terminate on that side of the palm, or else one on the side and one directly on the top of the palm under the pinkie.

This line is fairly straightforward. It appears on the hand of someone with psychic intuition.

I find it tends to be especially evident in the hands of clairsentients (people who psychically "know" things), although it may be found in the hands of folks with other psychic gifts.

There is still much more to examine in the area of psychic signs, but we'll save that for the next chapter. Next time, the other three psychic signs!

Chapter Forty-Five
Psychic Signs II

In our last chapter, we went over many of the issues surrounding doing a reading about a client's psychic ability.

We discussed the irony that psychic ability is so common in the human population (at least, latently); and yet knowledge and education about this ability is so uncommon.

The result is that you, as the client's reader, may be the first (and even only) resource she has to help her learn about and understand her gifts. We went into some basic ways you can prepare for this.

We went over how to determine whether one should review this area in a reading or not; and how to make it accessible for a client, based on her readiness to hear about her talents.

We talked about different types of psychic ability, which can be indicated by different landmarks or combinations of landmarks in the palm.

We compared psychic marks in both palms, and looked at what that had to tell us.

I listed the five markings of psychic ability. We briefly reviewed the first - the mound of the Moon (chapters 40 and 41), and we looked at the second - the Line of Intuition.

That was a pretty full chapter, but there's more to come.

Refer to Figure 10,"Psychic Signs".

It's time for the other three signs of psychic ability.....

In most areas of the palm, a "cross" or an "x" indicates conflict or competition, and is frequently a bad thing. A Mystic Cross is the exception to this rule.

Mystic crosses are "x" s or "crosses" located between the head line and the heart line. They stand for different varieties of psychic or mystic ability. There are three areas between these lines, each indicating a different area of skill. These areas are indicated on your handout with the notations "C1", "C2", and "C3".

The area indicated by "C1" falls roughly under the ring finger/pinkie. A mystic cross in this area indicates the gift of the psychic Artist.

This person is someone with the ability to channel music, poetry, or some other artistic endeavor. She has one or more individuals on the other side of the veil that are willing to work with her on this, if she wishes to do so.

She may not even be aware she has this talent, but still finds herself humming snatches of music or sketching pictures that just "pop into" her head....

She is good at influencing others.

She tends to be sensational, but not harmful to others.

She may be a bit superstitious.

The area indicated by "C2" falls roughly under the middle finger. A mystic cross in this area indicates the psychic gift of the Student of the Mysteries.

This person loves the Mysteries, whether they are spiritual, metaphysical, or just those funny things about the world that nobody talks about but that are true none the less.

She may be religious, or pursue Truth for its own sake.

She learns the Mysteries easily and joyously; sucking in knowledge like a sponge.

She uses what she learns; and explores new ways to use her knowledge.

Because of this, she is not only a student of the Mysteries, but also makes a fine teacher, researcher, or writer...

She is sometimes overly serious.

The area indicated by "C3" falls roughly under the index finger. A mystic cross in this area indicates the psychic gift of the Leader.

This person has the ability to lead and/or inspire people in a spiritual, metaphysical or self-improvement context. This is the mark of the priest, or the rabbi, or the mystic, or the guru, or the self-help guru (or, for that matter, the cult leader. These markings delineate skills without specifying if they're used for good reasons or bad ones.).

Her talent is not some kind of psychic mind control. It is rather the ability to reach out with her spirit to connect with the spirits of others in such a way as to enable them to face and embrace change in one or more of these areas (and we all remember from our discussions on the thumb back in Chapter 17 how most people find change challenging....).

This person has the ability to move people to learn, to grow, to make changes in themselves (hopefully for the better). She can empower people, or dis-empower them, based on her own nature.

Check her mound of Jupiter for self-esteem vs. ego.

Check her mound of Saturn to determine whether she wants to serve others, or be served herself.

Check the second mound of Mars for ethics and the ability to do what's right, as opposed to what's convenient or expedient.

These are some indications of what kind of leader she will be.

If her heart is in the right place, this person can be a positive inspiration to those around her.

In addition, this querant may be interested in or involved in the occult.

She'll sacrifice material rewards in favor of spiritual ones.

She tends to be a catalyst.

The fourth sign of psychic ability is the girdle of Venus. This landmark is a semi-circle at the finger edge of the palm. It runs from a point roughly between the index and middle finger, to a point roughly between the ring finger and the pinkie. To locate it, please consult Figure 10 on "Psychic Signs" and find the line marked "D".

The girdle of Venus indicates a number of things (sensuality, amongst others...). In the area of psychic ability, the girdle of Venus is a clear sign that your querant is an empath. (Here we are referring to the psychic form of empathy, as opposed to the psychological version, who is a person who has sympathy with your feelings....)

As mentioned briefly in the previous chapter, a psychic empath is a person who is really tuned in to the emotional vibrations of the people. This can be a positive gift or a massive burden, dependant on how well the empath manages her abilities and what is going on around her.

On the negative side, without good energetic shielding, an empath may have a hard time keeping other people's emotions separate from her own. Indeed, they can be overwhelming to her.

An angry or depressed person coming into the room she is in can drop her out of her previously happy state and into the other person's pain in a heartbeat. A conversational tone can sound like yelling to her, when augmented by the energy of someone in a rage. She may find large groups of people overwhelming, especially in stressful situations, such as the malls at Christmas.

She may get a reputation for being oversensitive. She is, and she isn't. She's sensitive to a fuller spectrum of what's going on, one that most people either don't experience or aren't consciously aware of.

There are even some empaths who appear to be mentally disturbed (most frequently appearing to be manic depressive or paranoid, for reasons which should be pretty clear) because they are so vulnerable to the emotions of others.

They're not, of course, but it's hard to find a psychiatrist who takes psychic abilities into account.

On the positive side, an empath who has good control over her gift, and can keep her emotions separate from those of others can use these gifts in many useful ways.

She's usually a good judge of character, and can sort out the phonies from the people she can trust. She can tell when folks are honest and when they're not. She usually can't be deceived unless she wants to be (in this case, she'll ignore what her gut is trying to tell her, usually to regret it afterwards).

She's good at negotiating things and mediating disputes. This is because she can feel the "vibes" for when people are dissatisfied or comfortable, which helps her reach a resolution that everyone can live with.

She tends to respect people and treat them kindly. Their happiness literally reflects back on her.

Some empaths are also expressive or radiant empaths. These folks can not only take in emotional energy, but also can radiate it out to those around them.

A radiant empath can make the place where she is feeling comfortable, safe, loving or exciting (to give only a few of the many possible examples). She can't control the emotions of others, but she can create a positive emotional cloud around herself.

In performance arts, a radiant empath can enrich her performance by using her gift as well as her voice or her body. In effect, she can "sing with her soul" as well as her mouth.

She can be good to work with. By setting an emotional tone, she can support whatever task needs to be done.

She can also be a lot of fun to hang around with.

Research indicates that empathy tends to be the most frequently expressed psychic ability in the human population.

Check both hands on your querant.
If there's no girdle of Venus, empathy is not her skill area.

If the girdle of Venus is darker in the non-dominant hand, lighter in the dominant, this person has potential that has either not awakened or that she's got locked down tight. Mention her sensitivity to emotions, let her know it's a psychic skill, and briefly talk to her about energetic shields (to keep her energy separate from those of others, so she's not overwhelmed), and some of the pluses and minuses of having this skill.

If it's darker in both, she's probably an active empath. Review this as you did for the developing empath. If she's overwhelmed, she may need input (probably more than her developing sister) on how to shield herself from others' emotions, and reassurance that there are positive aspects to this talent.

If there is a break or hole in the girdle of Venus, this is someone who was so overwhelmed by the gift that she's shut it down, whether consciously or unconsciously. (I see a lot of these kinds of folks).

Because empathy without the techniques to use it in a controlled fashion can be so overwhelming, there are many empaths who have the gift but shut it down. This gives them short-term relief, but robs them of the positive aspects of this talent (and many of them seem unhappy, or act as if they're living a life with something missing).

When an empath shuts her gift down, she may also find that this makes her able to cope during standard situations, but that she still is battered by the emotional vibes during higher stress times (whether the intensity of the situation overrides the shut down, or her own stress makes her more vulnerable to the vibrations around her).

For this reason, this shut down is a reasonable coping mechanism, but not a permanent solution to the challenges that come with psychic empathy.

This person needs to have the gift and the lock-down acknowledged as the best she could do at the time. She needs to know there are ways to manage this skill, so it can be a blessing as opposed to a pain. (It's good to know you have options, and since many empaths have had to go it on their own, they may not even know there are ways to work with their talent). It's good to tell her some of the positive aspects of empathy. (She probably is familiar with the negatives.) She

needs to have information on creating energetic shields.

Most of all, she needs acceptance that her gift is hers to use or not as she chooses. If she wants to develop shields and wake her talent up, that's fine; but when and if she does so are her business.

Your job is to give her the tools she needs to function as an empath, if she chooses to do so.

The fifth sign of psychic ability in the palm is called the Ring of Solomon. This landmark falls on the mound of Jupiter, underneath your index finger. It is not the line that circles the base of the finger but rather a ring falling below that line. To locate it, please consult Figure 10 "Psychic Signs" and look for the landmark labeled "E".

This mark only counts if it appears in both hands and if it is complete (touching the top of the palm at one end/the side at the other, with no gaps or breaks throughout) in both.

This mark is very rare in its complete and active form (although you may more frequently see partial rings, indicating a client is headed in this direction.....)

The complete and active Ring of Solomon is a sign of great psychic power. (My personal nickname for it is "Mucho Mojo".....) The person who has such rings has a large amount of psychic ability.

We've talked in prior chapters about how lines can change. If both rings appear in or complete themselves in your hands, it's the equivalent of being fast tracked from psychic kindergarten to psychic college.

Hopefully, your querant has the skills and technique to handle such power. Congratulate her on her achievement, and tactfully determine whether she knows how to work with what she's got or whether she needs a little guidance.....

This sign tends to appear when someone has been doing a considerable amount of work on her metaphysical abilities, enough to kick them into overdrive.

Which kind of markings go with which kind of abilities? It's not strictly speaking clear-cut, but there are some landmarks which are indicative...

All psychics have a well-developed mound of the Moon.

Empaths, of course, usually have a girdle of Venus (intact or broken...). They may also have a pronounced heart line, or a slanted head line.

Clairsentients (who "just know" things) tend to have a line of intuition, and may have a pronounced head line of any angle.

Clairvoyants (who "see" things), and clair-audients (who "hear" things) also have that line of intuition and the slanting head line. They both tend to have development in the mounds of Apollo, and/or Venus.

To differentiate between them, your clair-audient will also tend to exhibit development in the mound of Mercury.

(Can you figure out why those aspects would go with clairvoyance or clairaudience?

Think about it for a minute...

*

*

*

The mound of Venus covers aesthetics, which goes with visual and auditory people;

The mound of Apollo is arts and sciences, which overlap into both areas;

The mound of Mercury is communications, which is receptively an auditory skill;

And the line of intuition covers all of the intuitive arts.

You've already read about the more specified skills for the Mystic Crosses;

And, very frequently, two or more abilities will be combined in a single person (and therefore, her palm...), which means your reading will become more complex as you untangle one skill from another.

This concludes our overview of the psychic signs of the palm. Have your Rings of Solomon started to fill in yet?

In our next chapter, we'll be pulling together all of the factors we've learned to this point in order to do a more complete reading.

Hand Notes

After an underground period during medieval times, the Renaissance brought a resurgence of public interest in the art of reading the hand. Notable proponents of palmistry of the time included the orator Paracelsus and Robert Fludd, who wrote "Utriusque Cosmi Majoris Et Minoris Historica".

Chapter Forty-Six

The Complex or Complete Reading
(And the Targeted, Quick Reading)

In chapter Twenty Two, we went over the simple or basic reading; how to take all the information that you'd learned up to that point and organize it into a coherent, logical, step - by - step reading. That format translates into a good reading, which can give your querant a lot of basic, useful information....

But, you've learned a lot more since then......

This chapter is going to set you up with an organized framework to do a full reading, with all of the information, bells, and whistles that we've gone over up to this point. This is a map for visiting all of the lovely landmarks in the palm, without getting lost or driving down some back road or other....

Keep in mind, as I mentioned in chapter Twenty Two, this is only a set of guidelines based on what I've found logical and useful throughout the time I've been reading palms.

If you'd like to arrange things in another order, feel free.

If you'd like to look at some things and not at others, that's your prerogative (because Free Will Rocks!).

If your querant wants to go straight to love or finances, that's fine as well.

It's just good to have a basic order available to work with so that you don't inadvertently leave things out.

Here we go!

First and foremost, before you start the reading proper, you need to briefly review the concept of Free Will in regards to readings, just as you did before the simple reading (for more details, please see the section on Free Will back in chapter two...) .

Having this information makes the difference between a

reading being a party trick, or a powerful tool for having the best life possible. A decent reading reflects the life on its present course, but any querant can steer clear of a future he does not want by changing his course.

Once your querant knows this, he can take over his own helm..

People will usually ask you which palm you want. Give a brief explanation of hand dominance. (It educates them, which is a good thing; and helps you do the reading by alerting your querant why you'll need both hands accessible.)

Get that hand into its natural cupped position, if it isn't there already.

As we did in the simple reading, now it's time to get your bearings. While you do this, you'll probably be quiet. (One of the rare times that I am!), and it may feel like a very long time. Please don't worry - your querant will wait for you.

If it makes you or him more comfortable, you can say something like "Just a minute while I get in touch with your palm..." or something similar.

The basic information that's good to look at and become friends with before you start talking is the shape of the palm, the shape of the fingers, the thumb's flexibility (or lack of it), and whether your querant has a thumb chain or not. This gives you enough information for a substantial start to the reading, without being so much that you lose track of things.

Remember as you go along, you will not only be looking at landmarks, but also for markings such as islands or stars on those landmarks.

Once you've got your basic information, you're ready to start.

Start with the shape of the palm as the basic personality trait. (If round, you'll want to check the mound of Saturn to determine whether your querant has good boundaries or needs to learn to balance taking care of others with nurturing himself).

Go to the shape of the fingers as a characteristic that modifies the basic personality held in the palm. You may often find more than one shape of finger to be read.

Next, look at the thumb.

Read the flexibility for how your querant handles change.

Look at the thumb chain for stubbornness/persistence. (Remember to use tact. It takes a special or playful touch to tell a stubborn person he's stubborn, and make him like it...)

Next, we go into the factors of the simple reading that you learned in chapter Twenty -Two.

Look at the life line for life expectancy and the overall path of life. Remember to ask your querant if he wants to know his life expectancy. (This is one of the two scary issues - remember?).

Visit the head line for intellect, and the heart line for emotions.

Check out marriage lines and bracelets, as indicated.

From here, we go into the secondary lines.

Check the fate line for luck, money, and career. Comparing this line with the second bracelet can tell you how much the fate line is indicating luck and how much it is money. Watch for forks (for choices), breaks (for changes), and depth (for prosperity level).

Read the fame line for fame. (How much and when...)

View the health line for health or lack thereof. Note depth (for degree of health issues), time line, and compare palms to ascertain family influence on your querant's health.

Next, we visit the mounds.

Check the mound of Venus for sensuality and aesthetics. (Be careful with this- how much you say can depend on the querant's age, embarrassment quota, and whether there are children in the area.)

Review the mound of Jupiter for self-esteem, motivation, and leadership ability.

Visit Saturn for responsibility, personal boundaries, and balance between one's own needs and the needs of others.

See Apollo for Arts and Sciences.

View Mercury for business and communications.

At the mound of the Moon, see if there are psychic signs evident (prominent mound of Moon and/or any of the other signs noted in the last two chapters).

If such signs are present, you'll ask whether you can talk to your querant about psychic issues.

If he says no, focus on the creative aspects of the Moon.

If he says yes, review the psychic aspects of the mound of the Moon, as well as any of the other four psychic signs present (the line of Intuition, Mystic Crosses, the girdle of Venus, or rings of Solomon).

You can also cross reference for creativity with the angle of the headline.

To finish the mounds, check in with both mounds of Mars, for physical and emotional courage, or lack thereof.

By this time, you've gone over a great deal of knowledge, and your querant may be reeling from it all.

Ask him if he has any further questions or areas of concern. If he does, consult his palms to see if there are applicable answers there. If not, I'm going to give you two additional techniques (pendulum dowsing and straight intuitive work) in upcoming chapters that you can use to augment and support your palm reading for certain kinds of questions.

If he's got what he needs for now, your reading is complete.

I usually find it's a good idea to ask people if they're satisfied with their reading and wish them a pleasant day at this point, as it values them as individuals, and gives a clear end to the reading.

Of course, you're going to be using tact, courtesy, and compassion throughout the reading (as we've discussed many times previously), in order to empower your querant and give him information in a form that he can hear and benefit from. This makes a better reading for both you and your querant.

The points noted at the end of the chapter on the simple reading are even more applicable here.

Tell the truth, but be positive and empowering.

Make eye contact, smile, and be ready to listen.

Pay attention to your querant's face and body language, to get good feedback on whether you're doing a good job of presenting the information in the palm. (Review chapter twenty-two for some of the things this feedback can tell you, so you can give your querant the best, most individual reading possible).

Treat your querant as special and unique.

He is....

Every querant is..........

A full reading can take upwards of forty-five minutes to an hour, dependant on how many questions or issues your querant has, and how efficient you are.

Sometimes you don't have time for a full reading.

Sometimes you don't even have time for a simple, basic reading.

Maybe you're working at a fair or shop that does readings in fifteen minute blocks. Maybe your querant's budget is limited to a ten or fifteen minute block. Maybe the fair's closing down, and twilight is descending. Maybe you have someplace else you needed to be fifteen minutes ago.

For such times, the format you need is the targeted, quick reading.

To do a targeted quick reading, first it's good to acknowledge why you're not doing a full reading. Your querant usually knows the score, and knows there's a good, respectful reason why a full reading isn't an option (and reasons such as the ones above are good reasons.)

If he won't accept a good, respectful reason, it is all right to tell him you're sorry, but you cannot give him a full reading under the circumstances.

Once you're both on the same page, explain that, since there isn't enough time to get to everything in the palm, you want to make sure you get to what's most important to him. Ask him if he has a specific question or area of concern for you to focus on, or would he like you to look around in his palm and see what's interesting.

Many folks will want the general or "what's interesting" reading. In that case, look at the hand and see what jumps out at you.

If he has a specific question, you're well-enough acquainted with the palm by now to know where to go to address his particular issue. Most commonly, these will be love, money, career, or health.

Sometimes family will come up here. A palm is really more about the individual than their loved ones. The two supplemental methods we'll be looking at in upcoming chapters tend to be very useful in this situation.

When you're doing a quick reading (whether general or specific), it's important to remember to include positive information. In a full reading, there's usually plenty of empowering things, however in a quick reading, you're often directed to something the querant is anxious about.

Since you're only giving a small amount of information, it's crucial to be sure at least some of it is empowering...

If you are doing a bunch of quick readings for a group of people, it's worthwhile considering whether to give the initial Free Will lecture to the group as opposed to each individual.

It's still effective this way, and the time you save on repeating this crucial piece of information lets you do more or longer readings.

(It also gives people standing in line something to think or talk about....).

I've done it this way, and found it was a pleasant warm-up for the people waiting, as well as time-efficient.

One other thing to watch out for when doing a quick reading...

You're usually in the position of doing a quick reading because you don't have time to do more, whether due to your limits or those of others. It's not an infrequent experience, however, that your querant says he understands you only have ten minutes or five, but when that's done, wants more that you can't give.

Querants in this position are often masters of "one-more-thing".

You'll have to call this one as you see it. Sometimes you need to use more time to talk someone through an emotional crisis/catharsis. Sometimes he's willing to pay for another block of time and there's no one waiting.

Sometimes you can extend; but sometimes you can't.

If you do any significant amount of reading at all, you will come up against this situation. It's a good idea to prepare in advance how to politely, respectfully, but firmly say "No" in these circumstances. (Check your own mound of Saturn - how are your boundaries?)

I like to say that I wish I could help them further, but our time is up for now (and include any reasonable parameters, such as other people waiting, that have an effect on this.)

Short and sweet - that's how you want the quick reading.

This concludes this chapter on formats for the full reading, and the quick reading; and the bits and pieces appertaining thereto.

Hand Notes

The growth of scientific curiosity throughout the 18th and 19th centuries led to the restoration of the reputation of the reading of hands. The Victorian view of palmistry as a science caused it to be more widely accepted and openly practiced.

Chapter Forty- Seven

It's Never Too Late to Get the Most out of this Book
(and More Optional Homework)

Wow! You've covered a lot of material so far. You've learned about markings and mounds; and lines and other landmarks; and lots of different ways to speak the Truth and tie it all together.

Back in chapter Twenty -Three, I talked about ways you can get the most out of this book. Hopefully, you've been doing some of them, or even all of them as you've traveled through the chapters.

Then again, Life is Real, and Life is Earnest; and we all tend to have heaping piles of Things To Do on our plates.

So, maybe you haven't done the things you could to reap the maximum rewards from this book...

Know what? Free Will Rocks (and where have we heard that before?.....)

This means it's never too late:

Never too late to live your Dreams;

Never too late to have a Happy Childhood;

Never too late to try some of the things that will help you get the most out of this book!....

So, let's get busy!

In case you've forgotten chapter twenty-two, or the first half of this book has been carried off by pirates, here are six things to do to get the most out of this book:

1) Read the chapters. (One a week, or on any other schedule that works with yours.)

2) Look at your palm as you read the chapter to see what part of that chapter is live on display there.

3) Compare your palms (to see the difference between your potential and actuality).

4) Look at the hands of as many people around you as you can bring yourself to do. (The more you see, the more you'll learn.).

5) Practice, practice, practice!

And....

6) Have a go at the optional homework that's part of this chapter.

For those of you who've been working your way through these chapters, you've encountered the optional homework before. For those of you who are looking at things more randomly or have forgotten your last encounter with the optional homework (back in chapters twenty-three and twenty-four), here's a quick refresher.

The best way to learn how to read palms is to take in the information on what the various landmarks represent, and then go out and read as many palms as you can. The more actual experience you have, the more you'll learn, the faster you'll translate theoretical knowledge into actual skill, and the more comfortable you will get with the entire procedure.

That's in an ideal world,

But we don't all live in Utopia.....

Some people are not in a good position to practice on a lot of actual palms. There are lots of reasons for this.

You may be too shy to ask people.

You may be surrounded by people who are afraid or intolerant of metaphysical activities.

You may be short of time to get together with folks to read.

There are lots of reasons why the ideal learning set-up may not work for you.

The optional homework enables you to get some actual practice without volunteers or study-buddies. You can try it at your convenience, without having to co-ordinate with anyone else.

If you're in a situation where you can read actual palms, the optional homework can still be a beneficial additional way to enhance your learning process.

As previously stated, the optional homework is, like everything else in this book, optional. (That name's a dead give-away!). This means you do it and/or as many of the other options previously listed as you want to do, and can do in order to get the most out of this book.....

And no more....

Once again, I invite you to learn well, have fun, and become the best palmist you can within your interests, energy, life style, and other responsibilities, without making yourself crazy in the process....

So chose as much practice as works for you.....

Once again, we come to the audience participation part of the book....

Have you decided to try the optional homework? Go then to Figure 11, "Optional Homework II– Palm 1" and Figure 12, "Optional Homework II –Palm 2".

Are we all on the same page? Great!

Now, your new challenge is to look at each of these sample palms and determine as much as you can about the person you're reading.

Once again, we'll assume that these are dominant hands.

In our next chapter, I'll be reviewing the stories I find in the palms in question. See how our stories match up...

Hand Notes

People do not realize this, but engaging in a lot of psychic activity can be as much hard work as more physical endeavors.

If you're doing a lot of readings or very intensive readings, it's important to pay attention to what your body is telling you.

If you need to stretch, then stretch. If your mouth is drying out, then drink. If you're feeling tired, confused or woozy, take a break or stop for the day.

It's good to stretch your limits. Not so good to exhaust yourself. So pay attention, pace yourself and take good care of yourself, as you are taking care of others.

In all things, balance......

Figure 11 – Optional Homework II- Palm 1

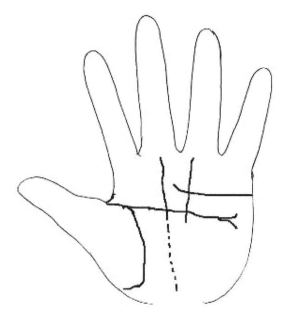

Figure 11 – Optional Homework II – Palm 1

Figure 12 – Optional Homework II- Palm 2

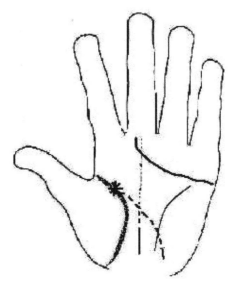

Figure 12 – Optional Homework II – Palm 2

Chapter Forty Eight

Optional Homework II-
The Advanced Palm - Some Answers

In our last chapter, we reviewed the many options you have to get the most learning possible out of this book. Once again, one of the options is the "optional homework 2" that came with that lesson.

The palms pictured are, of course, totally fictitious, and should not be confused with any actual people, whether living or dead,

So if you think one of them is you, you're wrong. I really did make them up.

Having got this far in this book, you're chock-full of a wide variety of palmistry insight and skill. (After all, to get this far required great motivation and focus. I'll bet your mounds of Jupiter and Saturn are amazing!).

Given that, I'm sure that even the simplest of glances at that handout has told you volumes.

But let's walk through it together, just for the exercise....

For structure's sake, let's start with some simple questions. Some answers will follow.

While looking at the handouts, do you pick up anything more than the answers to the questions? Please feel free to note these as before you look at the answers.

What do you see in these palms?....

Palm 1
How long will this person live?
How might this person prosper?
Will he be famous? When?
Will he be rich? When?
What characteristics does he have that will assist his career?

What are your impressions of this palm?

Palm 2

How long will this person live?

Have there been any note-worthy experiences in her life?

How are her finances? When are they good? When not so good?

How is her health? Physically? Mentally?

What kind of person is she?

What is your impression of this palm?

Palm 1-Some Answers

This person (allowing for free will) should live into his late 80s to early 90s.

His fate line indicates a shortage of money, although money is present throughout much of his life. When he approaches retirement age, his fortunes abruptly change for the better, and remain excellent for the remainder of his life.

This is often a function of someone who takes advantage of retirement to do something he really loves, and (in this case) is also highly successful at.

At the same time, his fame line indicates significant fame.

He has a writer's fork. It's not guaranteed, but this seems a likely road to fame and fortune for him.

In support of this, his level/logical head line will help him organize, and pursue his craft. (Given that the head line is almost dead level, he'll probably write non-fiction, rather than fiction.) You need a lot of focus to write productively, and well.

His short heart line indicates a private person, comfortable with working alone (an important prerequisite for a writer).

It's difficult to examine this on a handout, but a solid mound of Jupiter (for self- motivation), an optimal mound of Saturn (for being able to balance activities for yourself with those of others), an appreciable mound of Apollo (for Arts and/ or Sciences, depending on his topic) and a good mound of Mercury (for communication skills) would all be assets.

Palm 2 - Some Answers

This person (once again allowing for Free Will) should live until her early 80s (81 to 83 or so).

In her early 20s, she had a majorly traumatic experience (star on life line).

At around the same time, her health went from excellent to significantly impaired, although not invalided completely (middle level health line appears).

Her financial situation worsened soon thereafter in her late 20s/early 30s (fate line).

She has a great deal of energy, or chi (depth of life line); but problems with her physical health.

Check her non-dominant hand. If there are not similar health and fate lines; and if the star does not appear on her life line, the chances are good that this was an accident of some sort that impaired her health and ability to work.

Mentally, she's depressed (angle of head line). This is not uncommon with chronic disability. She's also distracted, and forgetful (depth of head line compared to length). Her depression and health problems may be distracting her from using her head, or there may be some kind of actual brain or mental damage here.

Besides being distracted and depressed, she's also very shy (length of heart line.) She is afraid to reach out to others, and therefore lacks the support of people that could help her better overcome the challenges she is facing.

Yet despite her depression and all of the challenges she faces, there is something in this woman that believes that things will work out for the best. She is depressed, but still, at heart, an optimist (upwards curve at end of heart line).

    Good for her!

    All of the information drawn from these two palms comes from things you've learned in the previous forty seven chapters you've gone through. (That's a lot of information!...)

    There's no doubt that some of these things just popped out at you when you first looked at the handout.

    More things may have become clear as you went through the answers I provided (and hopefully, the way that certain facts combine to yield further information made sense as I walked you through it.)

    If there are some things that still seem a little murky, referring back to the chapters in question can further augment what we found together in these palms.

    I'm hoping you're learning not only what the lines, mounds, and other landmarks mean, but how to look at them and think about them, so that they tell you a story about your querant, and what's beautiful and challenging and positive in her life.

    As a story-teller myself, I want you to be able to tell your querant's story.....

    This concludes our time with optional homework part II. Hope you're really beginning to see how things come together in a good palm reading.

    In our next two chapters, we'll be examining two different techniques that you can use to supplement a palm reading in certain circumstances.

    Catch you in the next chapter.

Chapter Forty-Nine

A Partner for Palmistry I-
Pendulum Dowsing

Palmistry is a wonderful, informative form of divination. It can give you an enormous amount of information about the person being read, including strengths, things he needs to work on, money, talents, past, future, and much, much more.

Sometimes, however, questions come up that are more challenging to answer through the palm...

Sometimes, a querant will have questions about family or friends. A palm is primarily concerned with the person attached to it, referring to other people primarily by how they affect your querant, so a question about his son's well-being may not appear in his father's palm.

Sometimes, your querant is looking for a very clear answer on a topic, and there are no specific indicators in the palm, or what information appears is ambiguous in regards to your querant's question.

Sometimes, a querant wants more information on a topic in his palm, but you've given him all the information the palm has to give.

What's a poor palmist to do?

This chapter and the one following it, will give you basic grounding in two methods of divination you can use to supplement a palm reading in such situations.

Before we go into specifics, it's worth noting that having supplemental techniques for divination does not mean that palmistry is inadequate, or incomplete. It just means it's better at some things than others.

I think of it as being like a tool kit. When you're putting up a building, if you want to drive a nail, you need a hammer. If you want

to screw something in place, you chose a screwdriver. Each is a perfectly
good tool perfect for its task, but not as good at the task of another tool.

There are many times I've read a palm without needing any supplemental methods. There are many times I've needed one.

It's all based on giving the reading that will meet the querant's needs, and empower him the most.

So, now we're going to put another tool in your toolbox.

On to dowsing.......

When folks think of dowsing, they tend to think of a man with a forked stick looking for water. Dowsing is that, but it's so much more.

There are other things you can dowse with besides a forked stick. You can dowse with "L-rods" which are a pair of metal rods shaped like the letter "L". You can use a pendulum. You can even dowse using your own body.

You can dowse for water. You can dowse for oil, or gold, or any other material. You can dowse for items that are lost (such as car keys).

You can also dowse for answers. Answers to questions that you or someone else has.

If you become fascinated with the various aspects of dowsing, there are lots of references and organizations out there that can help you learn more. We're just going to deal with some basics here.

We're going to look at dowsing for answers using a pendulum as a supplementary divination tool.

For divination purposes, a pendulum is a weight hanging from a cord/chain/other flexible item so that it can swing easily in any direction.

You can buy a pendulum. There are many for sale in new age,

gift, or rock shops. If you buy one, play with the ones available to find one that responds well to you. (This is a very individual thing).

You can use a familiar object, such as a necklace, to dowse with, as long as it moves easily in all directions.

You can even make one.

To make a pendulum, take a long, flexible item, such as a thread, a cord, a chain, a ribbon, or other similar thing.

Attach a weight to one end. Possible items include a pendant, a metal nut, a bead, etc; anything small with some weight that you can attach to your line. (My husband's first pendulum was a fishing lure on a length of line.). The important part is that it adds enough weight to facilitate a clear swing.

One additional, but optional step is adding something at the opposite end of your line from your weight, so you'll have something to make it easier to hold. This is a good thing, but not a necessity.

Now your pendulum is ready to work.

Where does the information a pendulum gives you come from? There's a variety of opinions.

Some say it comes from the pendulum itself;

Some say the pendulum helps you contact your own inner knowing;

Some say it puts you in touch with your higher self;

Others say the information comes from angels, or saints, or totems, or guides, or even the Divine Creator itself;

And it may well be any and/or all of the above.

For me, my pendulum acts as a friendly, positive, helpful little being all of its own self, but your results may vary.

If you get a pendulum, you might want to ask it....

Before you start asking your pendulum questions, you may wish to do some preparations first. There's a wide degree of opinions on this.

In a metaphysical universe, there's a large variety of beings and energies out there. Some are kind and benevolent. Some are not. Some are wise. Some are not.

It's kind of like the physical universe....

Because of this factor/because you are engaging in metaphysical activity/because you are going outside of yourself for answers, many people believe in doing some kind of preparation to ensure that you're getting your information from positive sources that have your best interests at heart.

Some people will pray.

Some people will dowse on questions such as these first:

- "May I dowse on this issue?"(Is it ethically o.k.?)
- "Should I dowse on this issue?"(Is it a good idea?)
- "Can I dowse on this question?" (Am I in the proper physical, mental, and spiritual shape to get an accurate answer?)

Some people will focus their intent on only receiving information from wise, good and positive sources whenever they do a reading.

Some folks do none of the above.

What do you do?

Follow your intuition, and do what feels right for you.

How do you hold a pendulum?

Whatever feels right for you.

Some people hold the cord pinched between the tip of thumb and forefinger.

Some folks hold it pinched between the tips of the thumb, forefinger, and middle finger (like a pen).

I like to hold the chain between the sides of my forefinger and middle finger. To me, it feels like not having it at my fingertips makes me less likely to unconsciously affect the pendulum swing.

You need to position the pendulum so it can swing freely. If the chain length would result in the pendulum banging into things, you can always take up a loop or two and wrap them around your fingers or hand, shortening the functional length of the chain.

You may also want to brace your elbow on a flat surface, such as a table. This prevents fatigue causing arm movements that affect your results (especially useful if you're doing a lot of pendulum readings, or if it's been a long day.) I usually brace, but it's not required of a person.

If you're reading for yourself, you're now set. If I'm reading for someone else, I like to position the pendulum over his upturned palm, in order to bring his energy into the energy field of the reading.

The above are options. I hope you'll try them, and chose the ones that work best for you.

Now that we've got the preparations down, in order to get you working with a pendulum, the first thing we do is set you up with a code between you and your pendulum for what is "Yes" and what is "No".

There are quite a number of movements a pendulum is capable of. Some sources use a generic response, such as "back and forth" means "yes", and round, and around means "no"....". My experience is that "Yes/No" can be different from person to person (referring to the readers), and even vary between pendulums.

So we've got to find out what your "Yes" is.

To do this, we're going to do a series of exercises that my husband calls "Mind-ups". (Kind of like sit-ups, without as much abdominal work.)

To start, after doing any preparations you chose, hold your pendulum so it can swing freely.

First, say "Show me Yes." (I tend to be polite, so I usually say "Show me Yes, please..." Feel free to be polite too, if you like.)

Note which way the pendulum swings. This is your "Yes"

Next, say "Show me No" (or "No, please")
How did it swing this time? This is your "No".

As to swinging, you have lots of options. There's forwards-backwards, left-right, clockwise circles, counterclockwise, and so forth.

For instance, my "Yes" is forwards-backwards (up-down, like nodding "Yes"), and my "No" is left-right (like shaking the head "No"). Your "Yes" and "No" may be a totally different combination.

The important thing is to find out what your code is. (Please note, with a different pendulum, you may have the same code or a totally different one. When you start a different pendulum, you need to check.)

Once you've got your "Yes", and "No", it's good to work through the remainder of the movements, as they may be needed to fill in under certain circumstances. (For example, if you need to walk as you dowse, a circular movement is more functional, and may emerge at that time.)

Say "Show me clockwise circles."
"Counterclockwise circles."
"Bigger movements."
"Stop, please."

The "stop" is very important. Sometimes, when you're getting large pendulum movements, it may be difficult to determine between one answer and the next without stopping in between.

When dowsing, it's not simply a question of "Yes" and "No". There's also the added factor of how big the swing of the pendulum is.

A "Yes" answer can be everything from "well, yeah......" (a very small swing) to a "Boy! Howdy! Absolutely, positively YES!!!" (a swing so large that it almost pulls the pendulum out of your hand).

A "No" answer can range from a "not really..." (tiny swing) to a "Never, ever under any circumstances!!!" (large swing).

So watch how much torque the pendulum's putting out, as well as the direction ("it don't mean a thing if it ain't got that swing....")

The pendulum is a limited divination tool, but a very good one, once you're familiar with it.

Its limitation is that it's primarily good for answering "Yes" / "No" questions. Because of this, half of the job with a pendulum is knowing how to use it, and the other half is knowing how to ask good questions in order to get a useful answer.

When you're using a pendulum, it may sometimes act oddly or "go all wonky".

Instead of a clear "Yes" or "No" swing, your pendulum may change from "Yes" to "No" and back again quickly; may jiggle uncontrollably; or may even stop dead still.

This is usually because you've asked a question that cannot be easily answered either "yes", or "no".

For instance, what if I was contemplating a job offer, and asked the pendulum if this would be a good job for me? If the job would make me tons of money, but also make me absolutely stressed out, the poor pendulum would have a hard time giving a good answer with only the options of "Yes" or "No".

So the pendulum goes "wonky" at that point.

And that's my cue that I need to ask the question another way...

Will this job make me rich?

Will it make me happy?

The secret is asking the right questions....

Once you've got your code down, the next step is to practice. Practice has less to do with "getting good" at the pendulum, and far more at building your confidence in it.

Start by asking answers to questions that you do know the

answers to.

Am I a woman?

Is my hair purple?

Is it raining?

Once you feel confident with working with the pendulum, you can go on to asking questions you don't know the answers to.

Will it rain tomorrow?

Will I be happy if I take this new job?

Will my querant's son finally get a job in the next six months?

Speaking of which, there's another way you can use a pendulum for divination, in addition to basic "Yes"/"No".

You can use it to set up a time line. Here's how that works...

Will I get a promotion at work? "Yes."

Within a year? "Yes."

Within 6 months? "Yes."

Within 3 months? "No"

You now know that (allowing for free will) the promotion is coming in between three and six months.

See how that works? Once again, asking the right questions.....

Using a pendulum for divination can be very helpful for supplementing a palm reading and answering questions not addressed in the palm, such as those listed in the beginning of this reading. This lesson gives enough information for you to begin utilizing this technique to empower your querants.

In the next chapter, we'll be discussing another divinatory method that you can use to supplement your reading, and get amazing results.

See you then.

Chapter Fifty

A Partner for Palmistry II -
Intuitive Readings

In our last chapter, we discussed the kind of questions and issues that can come up in a reading that may be challenging to address with the information in a palm. These issues include very specific information, areas where more than one resolution to a problem is equally likely, more information than is present in the palm itself, and information on a querant's family and loved ones.

We talked about the use of supplemental methods of divination to answer questions such as these.

I introduced the basics of dowsing with a pendulum for answers, and walked you through the steps of doing it yourself. We also went into variations of this, and the skills you'd need to be a competent dowser under the circumstances.

All in all, a fairly full chapter, giving you skills to fill in those open areas.

But, wait - there's more!

Let's journey now to the world of intuitive readings...

Why would you need to know how to do intuitive readings, anyway?

After all, you're full to the top with all of this great insight into palms. Failing that, you also now know how to use a pendulum to fill in any gaps.

So, why would I be taking you here?

I'm taking you here because the world is full of all different kinds of querants with all different kinds of needs. To fully serve them, you need an assortment of skills to meet each querant where she's at.

Many people will only need the self-insight a good palm

reading can give. Some will also need the additional clarity of the "Yes"/"No" information from a pendulum.

But some will need more......

Some will need the information that lies beyond any standard framework, and some will need you (or someone like you) to fly beyond those limits for them:

Because a good answer can sometimes be hard to find.

In the last chapter, we spoke of different techniques being like different tools in a tool box. Some are better for one job, and some are better for another.

Here comes one more tool for your toolbox....

As you know, in previous chapters, there were an assortment of ways to take in and integrate the basic techniques I was teaching.

You could simply read the chapter and think about it. You could look at your own hands, whether one or both, to apply the information.

You could use the diagrams in the optional homework to test your understanding of what you'd learned.

You could practice the reading techniques on someone you trust.

You could even publically announce you were learning palmistry or dowsing, and practice on any multitudes who volunteered to be guinea pigs.

In this chapter, however, your options are far more limited. If you want to go beyond theoretical knowledge, you're going to have to get an actual person to practice on in order to learn this. That's important, because the words on the page can't really go far enough to give you the scope of this method without actually trying it.

I can teach you how to do this, but you won't really understand it unless you do it:

So you need to go get yourself a partner.

Don't worry - I'll wait;

And I promise you that it'll be worth it...

Most methods of divination involve tools or structures that enable you to contact and use your innate psychic ability.

In an intuitive reading, we get rid of the "middle-man" and directly contact your psychic self.

It's kind of like flying without a net.

This can be a bit intimidating at first, because we have no cues or hints from the tool or technique to lean on. It can also be exhilarating because we're no longer limited by what's available to us in said tool or technique.

For instance, if you're reading cards, and what your querant really needs is a reference to an armadillo, there may not be an armadillo card available in your deck .(There may be, though. There's quite a variety of decks out there...)

In that case, your card reading may have a hard time getting at what the client needs, but your intuitive reading can go directly there.

Once you get the hang of it, intuitive readings can be very useful indeed.

Let's start with a basic method of doing an intuitive reading.

Your querant asks one of those questions that are challenging to read based on what's in the palm.

Your instinct tells you that it's a good idea to switch to a supportive method of divination.

The questions is more complex, so a simple "Yes"/"No" is not sufficient. This rules out pendulum dowsing as the best choice.

It's time to go intuitive.

You may wish to ask your querant clarifying questions at this point to specify the information he's looking for. (For instance, if he asks you "Is my son going to do well?", do we mean Money? Success? Happiness? Health?)

This is not because your own abilities are not sufficient to the task of answering. Rather, it keeps you from answering a different question than your client wanted an answer to.

If there are no more specific parameters (either because the querant isn't more specific, or because he doesn't wish to give you more information), that's fine. It just means that the answer received may be more free-ranging, and not necessarily target the querant's specific question. Your intuition may answer an important question that is not the question your querant asked.

Tell your querant that you're going to be doing a different kind of reading, and that it may take you a few minutes to get an answer. This is because, while you're focusing, you'll probably be silent. This can make a querant twitchy if he doesn't know you're actually doing something. (For that matter, you may find it makes you twitchy too. When I first started doing this, it seemed like it took forever before I received information....)

I like to say "Out of body-back in 5 minutes" in these cases.

I like to take the client's hands. This connects me more directly with his energy, and his question or concern, which helps me do this kind of reading better. In part, this is because I'm an empath. This has been effective for most of the people I've taught. You may choose to do this, or not.

Close your eyes, in order to screen out external distractions. This will help you concentrate better on what comes from within and beyond; and more clearly receive answers.

Focus your intent on receiving an answer to the question or concern you're working on. There are a number of things you can do to do this.

You can re-state the question out loud, or in your head.

You can think about the question.

You can form a solid belief such as "The answer to this question is coming to me now.".

Any of you who've worked with magick, metaphysics, or other

similar modalities can think of many other ways to focus intent.

When I'm forming an intent, I like to add the concept that the answer is going to come to me in as clear and understandable a form as possible.

This helps to cut down on appropriate, but wonderfully cryptic images (such as a bullfrog dancing the cha-cha....)

When your intent is ready, you either "reach out" for the information, or allow it to come to you. (To me, "reaching out" feels like reaching with my spirit, as opposed to my arm.)

Now, you'll start to get your answers...

You'll find that images start to come to you. These may be visual images, or things you feel, or sounds, or smells, or any other kind of input.

For some people, the images arrive almost instantly. For others, they take time to form. If yours do not arrive at once, take a deep breath, and relax. Know that the images are coming. Calm confidence brings the images to you more easily and quickly.

Don't get stressed. Just pay attention, and take note of the images you get to start out with.

When you've taken in one image, you can ask if there's any more. (For example, say "Next, please..."). Sometimes an answer consists of multiple pieces.

If an image is murky, unclear, or you can't understand it, it's fine to ask for help. (For example, say or think "Clearer image, please...")

When you're making these requests, you can do them in your head or out loud, dependant on your comfort level, that of your client, and the general circumstances you're doing the reading in.

Just take in the images first. Once you've got whatever it is that you receive, then you can go on to interpretation.

Before we get into interpretation, let's talk for a minute about symbols.

In many psychic modalities, such as intuitive readings or dream interpretation, you'll get images in one or more of your sensory systems (vision, sound, smell, etc.).

Sometimes an image is literal. As Freud said, "Sometimes a cigar is just a cigar...." In this case, what you see (or hear, or feel, etc.,) is what you get.

Sometimes, however, an image is a symbol of something else. That's when interpretation comes into the process.

There are lots of manuals out there on symbols, most commonly for dream work. They say a cat means this, and a pineapple means that, and wrap it all up for you clearly and easily.

These are lovely books. Unfortunately, they're neither accurate nor helpful.

We all stand at the center of our own Universes, with our own individual experiences. Because of this, when it comes to symbolism, each one of us has our own unique symbols.

For instance, a cat might mean loving acceptance to me, and indifference to you. These would both be legitimate interpretations of the symbol "cat", so which one was correct would depend on who was doing the psychic work.

To interpret a symbol (once you have one), the trick is to ask yourself the two magic questions:

"What is this symbol to me?"

And

"How did it make me feel?"

"What is this symbol to me?".....

For instance, take a bear....

Bears are large. They eat anything. They can be dangerous. They can be fast. They sleep all winter. They can be cuddly (like a teddy bear). They can be healing spirits. They come in threes (the 3 bears...)

"How did the bear make me feel?"

Frightened? Protected? In tune with Nature?

As you free-associate through these questions, you'll find answers within the list that jump out at you, giving you answers...

So a dream about being chased by a bear might be a warning of extreme danger to you, or a heavy message to me that I need to catch up on my sleep, or I'll face negative consequences.

And intuitive input works the same way.

See how that works?.....

Trust your intuition on whether the symbols you get are literal or symbolic. Your first impression is usually correct in regards to this. Use the literal images or symbolic interpretations to give your querant the answer to her question.

I find, many times I'm taking the information from those images, framing it in the context of the question, and pulling everything together as a story that gives her the answer in a way that's easy to follow.

It sounds difficult, but it's surprisingly easier than you'd think.

Go ahead - try it now with your practice partner.

I think you'll be pleasantly surprised....

You have your images.

You've consulted your intuition on whether an image is literal or symbolic.

What if you get an image that has no meaning for you either literally or symbolically?

When you do an intuitive reading, you usually receive the information in images that you interpret from a literal or symbolic standpoint. If the images are symbolic, they usually arrive in symbols from your own personal symbolic system. (For example, if a quilt symbolizes "comfort" to you, an image of a quilt indicates comfort....).

Sometimes, however, an intuitive reading will bring up images that are meant directly for your querant. In this case, she is supposed to be an active part of the work, rather than receiving your interpretation passively.

There are lots of reasons that this can be important. Thinking images through can trigger active insight, or response from your querant. Sometimes she needs to hear something totally outside of your symbol system (for example "toucan"). Sometimes hearing something that obviously makes no sense to you, but means everything to her can emphasize the reality, and importance of this reading.

If you get an image that makes no sense, here's where you need to step up to the plate. You may fear looking foolish, but, if you're going to fully serve the person you're reading for, you need to move past that.

Ask your querant "Does _____ mean something to you?" (The blank is your image.)

If it doesn't immediately ring a bell, it may be something they haven't thought of at the moment. (I've had many readings where the querant draws a blank at the time, but tells me at a later encounter that the answer "popped into her head" later that evening.)

It may also be symbolic (trust your intuition on this one) but, in that case, it'll be symbolic in <u>her</u> symbol system.

Ask the magic questions.

"What is _____ to you?"

And

"How does _____ make you feel?"

Take the answers she gives you, and draw your interpretation from them.

To give an example, I once did a reading for a woman who wanted to know if she should take a former boyfriend back into her life. There were no clear indications in her palm, and my gut told me

an intuitive reading was indicated. When I closed my eyes, the only image
I got was of a birdhouse.

Huh?

A birdhouse had no meaning to me, literally or symbolically. I was relatively new to this technique and somewhat nervous about looking foolish, but I took a deep breath, and said "Does a bird house mean anything to you?"

"No!" she said. My heart dropped into my boots.

After a pause (which seemed like eternity), she said "I have a bird house...."

"Yes....." I said.

"He made it for me..."

I said "and...."

She said "It fell down awhiles back....."

"mmmm?......"

"I haven't gotten around to putting it back up yet."

"There's your answer!" I said. "You're not ready to bring him back into your life, anymore than you were to give house space to the birdhouse he made!"

She smiled, and her face relaxed in response to this answer. It made sense to her.

Although this process was stressful for me and seemed to take forever, the results were ideal in this situation. If I'd given her a straight "yes" or "no", it wouldn't have meant much to her, but by walking together through the image given and how that resonated with her own underlying beliefs, she was part of and received information that was far more meaningful and helpful to her in understanding where her best interests lay.

She had to be part of the process in order to get the answer she needed.

It's worthy of note that, while this seemed to take a long time, the more times that I've done this, the quicker and easier it's become.

An intuitive reading is good in a number of cases.

It's good for supplemental information about people associated with the querant you're reading (as a palm tends to be mainly about the person themselves.)

It's good for additional information beyond what's in the palm.

It's good for "What can I do to best change the path I'm currently on, as reflected in my palm?"

It's good for weighing two equally likely options.

You can ask "What do I most need to know right now?"

Finally, one of my favorite applications is, at the end of a reading, to focus my intent to determine what will be my querant's most likely life lesson for the next six months. It makes a nice completion to the reading.

This completes the overview of the basic steps for doing an intuitive reading. The best way to understand it fully is to get out there and practice, practice, practice!

We've done fifty chapters about taking care of your querant.

Our next chapter focuses on taking care of the psychic....

Chapter Fifty-One

Sustaining the Psychic

We're nearing the end of an incredible ride. You've had 50 chapters (almost a year's worth, if you do one per week) on how to best take good care of the clients, friends, and family who come to you for a good palm reading.

Now I'm going to take a different turn.

This chapter is on how best to take good care of yourself.

This chapter is important for several reasons. First and foremost, we are all unique, special children of the Universe, and deserve to be treated with care and respect. When you take good care of yourself, rather than waiting for someone else to do it for you, you take command of your own health, wholeness, and well-being. That is a powerful, beautiful thing.

Secondly, when you are whole, healthy, and feeling good about yourself and the world around you, you're in far better shape to help others. This includes giving better readings.

Let's go look at factors that will help to keep you in your happy space.....

Everyone (as we've said before) has Free Will. Everyone, therefore, is unique, with his own particular desires and needs to be met in order to be his best.

I'm going to be going over a number of areas to consider in order to keep yourself nurtured and in good shape to do readings. I'll tell you what different people think on the subject, and what my own personal experiences have been.

As they say in commercials, your results may vary.

I'd encourage you to consider each of these areas yourself. Consider my input and that of others in each area, but resolve an area by what works best for you personally. By doing this, you'll have a plan that works best for you.

That's what counts.

Some people meditate before they do a psychic reading. Some people even feel it's necessary to do a certain amount of meditation (2 hours, for example) before they feel they're in a good space to read.

Some people don't.

I tend to incorporate a certain amount of meditation, self-hypnosis, and other altered state work informally throughout my life, but I don't find it necessary for myself to follow a structured program of meditation prior to reading. I use my routine, certain practices (such as smudging with sound), and my overwhelming desire to be of service to put myself in the proper mental/spiritual framework to read.

On the occasions I haven't been able to get there, I don't read if I can't get myself in the right space. I do find that an expectation that it's easy to get myself into that proper head space goes a long way to actually making it easy though. (Use that self-fulfilling prophesy to help you!)

If you need or want to meditate or otherwise prepare, it's fine to do so.

Some people can work under challenging physical conditions. Some people can't.

Physical challenges can include temperature, outdoor settings, weather, noise, air quality, onlookers, psychics packed in closely together, and other such circumstances.

In my history as a reader, I've had to read under quite a number of challenging circumstances (for example: close quarters, loud rock music, surrounded by creatures from horror films, and so on).These circumstances seem to have built me into a rather resilient reader. Due to my asthma, I have problems with too much incense or other scented items, but am otherwise fairly tolerant of challenging set-ups, and can read under most conditions.

There are worse things that stretching your comfort zone.

It's a good thing to know what the physical set-up will be before you arrive, so you can plan for things that might be problematic.

Will you be outdoors in cold or wet? Dress in layers, and bring extra dry socks.

Will the area be loud? Ask to be positioned away from the monster speakers, and use a smaller table so you don't have to shout as far.

Will you be in a room crammed full of psychics? Go early, and get an edge position for some breathing space.

Plan your circumstances to be as comfortable as possible, but don't be afraid to stretch outside of your comfort zone.

You might surprise yourself.....

Much of the time, you'll find yourself reading in a space that is not your own. This means that any number of people may have passed through this space or lingered there. Each of these people has his own attitude and concerns, and each has contributed to the energy you'll find in that space when you get there.

The results are energy - stale energy, negative energy, bright shiny energy; and it's all yours to work in!

Because of this, some people do energy clearing. Some don't.

You can "smudge" using burning sage. You can "smudge" using sound (ex: clapping hands to get stuck energy moving). You can clear a space using your intent, or by visualizing light cleansing it.

I like to clear energy using a Tibetan singing bowl. I circle the space clockwise to build good energy (although you can go counter-clockwise to banish bad), and I circle three times for emphasis.

As I sing the bowl, I focus my intent that "There are good readers here. There are people who need what we have. May they find us. May we read wisely, and well, giving people the information they need to have healthy, happy, prosperous lives. May they prosper. May we prosper. May all be for the highest good of all concerned in the name of all that I hold sacred."

You're free to use my statement of intent, or create one of your own.

Be aware that if you're working in someone's home space, your clearing the energy may seem insulting or hurtful to them. (After all, you're saying their energy is less than ideal.). Judge such a situation carefully in order to be respectful. (One option is to use a quiet, internal visualization for clearing energy.)

I find that making a habit of clearing when I start helps to automatically put my head into the space of "ready to read now".

One of the more important environmental factors in reading palms is light. You need good light, or you won't be able to see the full nuances of the palm.

I've read in half-light and twilight. It tends to give one a headache, and make a good reading more difficult.

If you're reading in some place that you're not familiar with, it's good to check in with the owner/co-coordinator in advance, and emphasize that you need good lighting to really do your job. If this person knows in advance, she can choose to seat you directly next to the best light source. You can also bring a battery lamp to augment available lighting.

I've also found a couple of additional resources for this. At a truck stop, I picked up a tiny flashlight designed to fasten with Velcro to your finger for a rave party. Since many time, I'm using my index finger to point at what I'm looking at in a palm, this directs the light perfectly.

In a fabric store, I picked up an embroidery magnifying mirror that rests against my chest suspended from a strap around my neck. In the mirror are small lights. You can position the palm directly under the lighted, hands-free mirror. This gadget will enlarge the lines, and illuminate them for you as well.

It's still better to start with good lighting.

They say that, in Life, position is everything. Let's talk about position next.

If you're doing a casual mini-reading or two at a party, a casual position is fine. If, on the other hand, you're at a fair or shop, and you're expecting to do multiple readings over a prolonged period of time, it's crucial to have comfortable, good positioning for your back, neck, legs, and every other part of your body. If you don't, you can end up with aches, pains, or even strained muscles. A little bit of thought and planning can prevent this.

It's also important for your client to be positioned comfortably. Good positioning makes a reading a more pleasant experience and helps her concentrate more on what you're telling her. Bad positioning can negate everything you're bringing to the table.

Let's start at the bottom, and work our way up. First you need a comfortable chair at the proper height for your feet to reach the ground easily while you sit. If you're going to be sitting for any extended time, it's better for the chair to be cushioned, as hard chairs can make portions of your anatomy fall asleep.

The depth of the chair (from chair back to front of the seat) should be the right length to fit your thighs so your back reaches the chair back. If the depth is too deep, you'll slouch to rest against the seat back, and that will make your back hurt.

Once you've got a good chair, you need a good table. Because you spend a good amount of time leaning forward, and holding your client's hands with your elbows on the table, the ideal table is the right height to rest those elbows comfortably, without slumping or straining. Some tables come with adjustable height, so you can set them for your best level.

Your table should be deep enough that you and your querant can hold hands, and both rest your elbows. If either of you have to stretch, or you can't rest those elbows, one of you will be uncomfortable.

A tablecloth on the table is not only attractive, but also makes the table more comfortable to lean on.

You can place items on your table for decoration or use, but be sure there's a clear area in the center large enough for the circle of two people's arms.

For your querant, a comfortable chair is also important. I encourage my clients to "scoot up" to the table before we start the reading, in order to prevent strain or discomfort.

Finally, before you decorate your table, consider its position in regards to available light, as we discussed in the previous section. If you have to hunch or lean to get into the light, you may wish to realign your table.

While we're talking about body positioning, let's talk about the body itself. If you're doing a lot of readings in a row, it's very easy to lose track of what your body needs. This can end up throwing you out of balance and interfering with your ability to do a good reading.

You need to listen to your body.

You need to drink liquids, before you start feeling parched or dehydrated.

You need to eat meals, or at least snacks, as your body needs them.

You need to listen to your muscles, and stand up to stretch as needed.

You need to have clothing layers that you can put on or take off as you need. (Heavy psychic work can interfere with your ability to maintain your body temperature.)

You need to make time to visit the bathroom. (It seems odd to have to say this, but it's something that I hear repeatedly from psychics doing back to back readings).

If you're doing a lot of readings, you may find yourself getting light-headed, slurring your words, or feeling slightly intoxicated. (How much is a lot varies from person to person.) In this case, you need to do something to ground yourself.

And if you can't remember to do these things, you may need to get yourself a buddy who will remind you to do them.

In busy situations, you may feel that you're holding up the clients waiting if you stop to drink, stretch , or visit the facilities. You are a little bit, but my experience is most clients are glad to give you a brief break to take care of yourself, as long as you're polite about it. Most of them are kind and caring people anyway, and all of them want you at your best when you read for them.

Remember to listen to your body. If you listen, it will tell you what it needs.

To do a good reading, you need balance in your energies. You need that spiritual/metaphysical connection to draw your information from beyond. You also need the grounded connection to physical reality to be able to focus, pay attention, and speak clearly.

When you do psychic work, you're connecting with energies outside of the material. If you're doing a lot of readings at once, you may find your connection with your body and the physical world not as strong as it normally is. You may feel spacey, slur your words, feel drunk or less coordinated. This is because, as you strengthen your energetic/spiritual connection, your connection with your body becomes weaker.

This is the point you need to do some grounding work.

Grounding practices are things you do to strengthen your connection with the physical world.

There is a wide assortment of things you can do to ground.

You can do something physical, such as get up and take a walk, or dance vigorously.

You can eat something. (Some specifics are in the next section.)

You can stomp your feet.

You can hug a tree or a building's metal support pillar.

You immerse your hands in running water, or take a shower.

The important thing is to be prepared to do something grounding if you start to feel "fuzzy" while you're doing readings, or after you finish.

Being ungrounded can not only interfere with doing readings, but can also make you incoordinated, and interfere with your ability to do things such as drive safely. It's wise to have several options that work best for you to ground yourself, and be prepared to use them when you need to.

To do your best job as a reader, you need to be firmly balanced between Heaven and Earth. Grounding helps with this.

What you eat and what you drink can have a major effect on how well you can function as a psychic. It can make you spacey or grounded, competent or overwhelmed, exhausted or raring to go.

Food and drink are one of the major areas where your results may vary. I'm going to give you some of the theory on this, as well as my own personal experience, but the bottom line truly must be to try these things yourself, and find out what works (and what doesn't) for you personally.

To start, it's important to stay hydrated when you read. Not only will your lips and tongue dry out physically if you're talking a lot during readings, but also dehydration will harm your focus, concentration, and ability to interpret signs and symbols accurately.

It's good to have a good supply of your chosen beverages within arm's reach before you start reading. This lets you drink while you read, rather than having to go find something. You are also more likely to remember to drink, if your liquids are right there.

Overall, the ideal thing to be drinking is water as it is the body's buddy. I like it cold, as I find it both tastier and more refreshing that way. A human being is already Nature's way of moving water from place to place, so why not help the process along?

If the environment is hot, or you're planning on doing a lot of readings, sports drinks can be helpful. I find multiple readings can be as wearing as physical exercise, so replenishing your electrolytes can keep you going.

Some folks feel that caffeine can interfere with energetic or metaphysical activity. I find the right amount of caffeine can keep me energized and in balance between cosmic contact and well-grounded. I drink cola (particularly vanilla cola) and, when the going gets particularly tough, mocha cappuccino type drinks.

Speaking of caffeine, let's talk chocolate. Some people (the same ones who avoid caffeine in general, no doubt) think chocolate interferes with psychic work. Some people feel it makes them too "spacey" to focus and read at all.

For me, chocolate is a wonderful energizer and grounding food that puts me in the balanced state I need to work. (I think that chocolate grounds me because the tongue is in the body, and I can't taste chocolate without it!) I prefer dark chocolate's "more bang for the buck" flavor. I find Mexican chocolate convenient to carry in my psychic's kit because (lacking dairy) it doesn't melt as easily as regular chocolate.

In addition to chocolate (the cocoa) being grounding, I've also found references indicating that sugar can free you of the overwhelmed feeling a psychic person can get, and that butter can slow down over-sensitivity so you can cope better with the input you're getting (picture controlled input coming in more slowly.)

No wonder I love it! (Your results may vary, so try it for yourself.)

In regards to other foods, some people believe that one must eat a vegetarian diet to function at one's best psychically. Other people don't believe this. I listen to my body and eat what it wants, which includes meats and vegetables. The presence of meat in my diet does not seem to harm my ability to do readings, and my research indicates that meat, and oily foods such as chips can be very grounding.

When I'm preparing for a heavy day of reading, I tend to pack a little survival kit including an assortment of caffeinated and non-caffeinated beverages, including water; chocolate; and salty snacks such as crackers, pepperoni, or string cheese. Keeping it close to me makes it more likely that I'll hydrate regularly and grab appropriate snacks to keep me energized and grounded as I go along. I also tend to start with a solid breakfast (including meat and cheese, as well as carbohydrates).

After I finish a day of heavy psychic work, I listen to my body, and have a solid meal based on what my body wants. (Sometimes it wants meat, sometimes heavy carbohydrates, such as pasta, and always chocolate...). This grounds me, and brings me fully back into this world.

From what I can see, what each psychic needs to eat and drink to be at her best varies widely. To find the ideal diet for you, I'd recommend that you make a personal investigation of options such as those listed above, and decide what works best for you by trying things, and listening to what your body tells you about each one.

Are you doing a lot of readings? Do you feel spacey, confused, exhausted? Is there a line out the door, and you can't take it anymore?

Well, take a break!

Many readers are caring, giving people who can't stand to abandon someone in distress. That's a beautiful thing, but even the most puissant reader will hit the wall eventually, and when that happens, your readings go downhill.

You can recharge yourself, and go on if you take a break. Even better, take a break earlier, pace yourself, and don't hit that wall at all.

A break can be a walk around the building. It can be a one minute beverage stop. A break is whatever your body needs to reset.

The problem is how do you face the next person in line, and say you need to break now?

Actually, most clients are surprisingly good about this. Most people who come to psychics are caring, giving people themselves, and want you to be o.k. Furthermore, most of them will want you in good shape so you can do your best reading for them.

I find that, as long as I'm polite, most people are glad to be gracious. Excuse yourself to visit the facilities. Say you need to stop and drink so you're hydrated. Make a joke about your late lunch. If you're respectful, they'll respect you right back.

So listen to your body, and take a break as needed to keep yourself on an even keel

----

Finally, keep in mind that it's o.k. to say "No!"

"No" to the uber-skeptic who's loudly proclaiming that all psychics are frauds.

"No" to the clean-cut guy who somehow gives you the creeps.

"No" to "one last reading" when your brains are already running out of your ears.

Trust your intuition on when it's right to press forward, and when you're "stick-a-fork-in-her-she's" done.

You aren't required to read for the World, unless you want to.

It's very important for you to remember to take care of yourself, in and amongst taking care of everyone else. Self-nurturing will make you a stronger, healthier psychic who gives better readings for the people around her.

And that's a beautiful thing.

In our final chapter, we'll be looking at where you'll take this knowledge, now that you have it.

<u>Hand Notes</u>

The optional homework is one really good way to practice what you've learned and improve your palmistry skills. Want to know some others?

1. Let family and friends who are supportive of these kinds of interests know that you're learning to read palms
2. Find a study buddy who also wants to learn.
3. Look for charitable events, such as marathons, who'd like additional activities
4. Mention you're learning this at parties. Watch folks scramble to sit next to you.
5. Start a lunch-time mutual practice group.
6. Have friends corral their friends for you to practice on.
7. Mention you're learning this in casual conditions, such as non-busy check-out lines. Watch the hands stick out…
8. Got friends interested in metaphysical and alternate health practices? Stage a party where each of you explains and demonstrates a bit of your area.
9. Look for still pictures of palms in magazines and on the internet.

There are lots of opportunities to practice palmistry waiting for you, and lots of people who'd love to help you practice.

Chapter Fifty-Two
The Road Ahead

We've come full circle. You started with what you knew about divination and palmistry and we've walked together through all the information, skills, and techniques I use to read palms.

So now it's time to take this information, and make it your own.

If you recall, back at the beginning in chapter one, I asked you to go through this course, but to listen closely to your own intuition. I recommended that you take only what speaks to your wisdom, and leave the rest. Regardless of what you take, and what you leave, you'll find that what you take will work for you.

I also recommended that you add other things from other sources that speak to you, as long as these things don't contradict what you're already doing.

Finally, it's been my experience that those of my students who actively use what they've learned to read palms will start finding things of their own to add to this body of knowledge. That's also good.

For instance, one of my students has gone on to read palms professionally. He will often touch base with me to tell me that this or that technique I taught him is very convincing, moving, or astonishing to his clients.

The only thing is that frequently the method he's so enthusiastic about is not one I taught him. It's something that's just come to him.

I laugh when I hear this. It's very flattering that he believes that a good idea must have come from me, but it's so much more impressive to me to have the evidence that palmistry is a living, growing modality, and that a person's intuition will lead him to new truths if he trusts it.

So, trust your intuition. Take what speaks to you. Leave the rest. Add what sings for you.

And make the system your own....

As you read more and more palms, you'll begin to develop own style of doing it. You may change the order, or focus on different features than I do. It's all good.

You may find that you notice markings or combinations of landmarks that appear consistently with certain issues or types of people. These may be indicators that are not part of what I've taught you. That's fine. I know a lot but I don't know everything there is to know (I don't think that any human being does.)

Stay alert for these distinctive combinations. Many times, you'll find them because you'll need them. It's been my observation that different kinds of readers tend to draw different varieties of querant. If you're reading a lot, the odds are good that you'll be given the tools you need to do the job you're here for.

When I read, I have certain phrases, stories, and jokes that I use for particular combinations of features or situations. I've shared some of them in the body of this book. I've developed them over the years because, for me, these particular words have turned out to be the best way to help a querant hear and understand a concept, and empower her to address it.

My words work for me. If they work for you in a reading, you're welcome to use them; but you may find that you need different ways of saying things to empower your querant. I'd recommend that you keep an eye on the things that you tell a client, and, if you find a turn of phrase that really works for one querant, you save it away for when you may need it again.

The right words at the right time can make a world of difference.

Sometimes you'll do a perfectly good reading and your

querant will not connect with it.

She'll say "I'm not stubborn".

She'll say "I don't have any plans to go into business."

She'll say "That doesn't make any sense to me."

For most readings, your input will trigger a connection immediately (what I think of as a "Cosmic A-ha!"). Sometimes, however, the querant needs to go home and think about it before the pieces all fall into place.

Sometimes, too, the things your reading is referring to only become clear later on. I've had many people shake their heads confusedly, but see me six months later and tell me that the reading all came true.

If your querant is looking confused or saying your reading makes no sense to her, you may feel tempted to waffle, or revise things so you don't look foolish or wrong.

I'd recommend against that. Don't push the point. (That's arrogant, and makes you look uncertain.) Just politely say that sometimes certain elements in a reading may make more sense later on. After saying that, move on to the next part of your reading.

Trust me - it'll work out.

The more you read, the more you'll start to get "extra" knowledge. Things that aren't actually strictly speaking in the palm....

Remember back in chapter 50 where I talked about intuitive readings? It's kind of like that, except you won't close your eyes and reach out for it. You'll just get an impression....

An impression that a person who looks happy is actually depressed;

An impression that someone is deceiving your querant;

An impression that you need to say "cumquat" to this querant.

At this point, you may hesitate, or worry that you'll look like a fool if you say this thing from out of nowhere. Don't worry. That flash of intuition is usually there because there's something your querant needs to hear that isn't covered by the standard features of the palm.

Take a deep breath, and center yourself. Say "Does _____ mean something to you?" (The space is for whatever intuitive information you received).

Remember that this information may be literal or symbolic, just as it is in intuitive readings. An image of a bird in a cage can be a literal pet, or symbolic of a lifestyle that feels like a trap.

Trust your intuition. The more you trust it, the stronger it'll grow...

There's some little debate in the world of psychic phenomena about whether you should charge for readings or not.

Some people believe that it takes extraordinary talents; and of course you should charge for it.

Some people feel that it's a spiritual gift - that you're just the vessel for something greater working through you; and of course you shouldn't charge for it.

I fall in the middle of the discussion.

I do believe that psychic ability is a spiritual gift. I also believe that skills at dancing, teaching, or building buildings are also spiritual gifts. I believe every one of us has talents peculiar to ourselves, and that our talents are given us by the divine Creator.

No one would have a problem with someone being paid for those other talents. I believe that a person who has worked hard at becoming a skilled and compassionate reader is as deserving of recompense as any other person who develops her gifts.

That being said, I also believe that people have a right to share their talents for a reduced rate or free if they so chose.

If you chose to charge for readings, I'd encourage you to neither undervalue nor overvalue your work.

The reader who cuts her rates to the bone sends a message of uncertainty, desperation and poor self-esteem to her clients and herself, which can interfere with her ability to read and the client's confidence in the reading.

The reader who charges rock-star prices tends to price herself out of the field, and not reach the clients who really need her skill.

Charge a reasonable rate, based on what's appropriate to the milieu you're working in. If you see someone in dire distress, you can always cut a special deal if it seems appropriate to you.

If you chose to read for free, be sure you balance your needs with the needs of others. Know how to say no to protect your own energy, and to prevent others from becoming dependant on you and trying to make you responsible for their lives. (This happens more frequently when you give free readings).

It's also good to avoid undercutting other readers who charge a fee. (You may have a day job, but the psychic down the way may give quality readings, and need to charge in order to pay her rent...)

This is an area there are many different right answers. Trust your intuition on what's the right thing for you to do.

Finally, practice, practice, practice!...

There is nothing on earth that will make you a better palm reader than doing it. Doing it a lot!

Let people know you are learning this, and you'll have a slew of people who immediately stick their hands out, eager to be your guinea pigs. Everyone will want to sit next to you at parties. People will start introducing you to other people you've never met before who'd also love to have their palms read.

You'll circulate like crazy.

Another way to practice is volunteering for benefits. I've done quite a number of events raising money for charities, premiering books, and at local festivals. Even if there's no pay involved, there's lots of lovely practice (and the opportunity to get your face out there, and your business cards and flyers into the hands of people which may lead to paying gigs later on, if that's what you want...)

The more you practice, the better you'll get - and the better you get, the more opportunities you'll get for practice.

In closing, I'd like to encourage you to take what you've learned and use it.

For some unknown (at least to me) reason, palmistry has become a dying art. While there are plenty of books on the subject, there are relatively few actual palm readers in circulation, and, unless things change, there will be fewer and fewer as time goes on.

This is one of the reasons I started teaching palmistry in the first place. I appreciate and value a good reader of Tarot or other methods; and I want palmistry to continue to have a place alongside of these other ways of empowering people.

I've had many students tell me that they couldn't learn palmistry from books, but could learn it when I taught them. In my classes, I break palmistry down into simple steps, in order to make it easier to learn and understand. This book follows that path. It is my wish that people will be able to learn from this book, and that my book will go many places that I cannot.

If you find that palmistry speaks to you;

If you find that you enjoy it;

If you find you have a gift with palms for helping others empower themselves;

I hope you'll take the information in this book, and make it your own.

Use what speaks to you, and leave the rest;

Add your own symbols, and methods;

Read ethically, and with love;

And remember that every querant is unique, and special, and worthy of your respect.

I wish you well. Blessings on your Adventures in Palmistry to come....

Glossary

<u>Bracelets (also known as Rascettes)</u> - lines on the wrist indicating health, wealth, and happiness. Good for doing a quick mini-reading.

<u>Break</u> – a break in a line where the line continues afterwards. Indicates a change in direction with two or more equally likely possibilities.

<u>Chain</u> – marking on lines in the palm that looks like the links of a chain, as in a necklace or bracelet. Indicates challenges.

<u>Clairaudience</u> - receiving information psychically through the sense of hearing.

<u>Clairsentience</u> - receiving information psychically through "just knowing" things.

<u>Clairvoyance</u> - receiving information through the sense of sight.

<u>Cross</u> – marking looking like a cross or x; warns of opposition.

<u>Empath</u> - a psychic who is very sensitive to people's emotional vibrations. Can be receptive only; or both receptive and projective/radiant.

<u>Feathering</u> - a line with a series of little branches along its length, making it look like a feather. Frequently indicates scattered energy in the characteristic that the line represents.

<u>Fork/Branch</u> - where one line splits into two or more divisions. Divided energies.

<u>Free Will</u> - the divine gift that every person is given of the ability to make choices, (whether good ones or bad); and, by choosing, control (to a certain extent) the kind of life that he or she has.

<u>Girdle of Venus</u> – loop straddling the bases of middle and ring fingers; sign of psychic empathy.

<u>Grid or Grille</u> - a marking where multiple horizontal and vertical lines overlap, resembling the mesh in a screen door. Indicates challenges or opposition.

Island - a mark where a line splits apart, and then rejoins itself again, forming a closed loop. Indicates confinement.

Landmark - a structure or location on the palm.

Mounds - the bumps or raised areas on the palm.

Mystic Crosses - "X"s in specific locations on the palm that indicate particular types of psychic ability.

Palmistry - the art and science of reading palms.

Querant - a person receiving a reading (from "query" meaning "question"). The querant is the person with questions to be answered .

Ring of Solomon - landmark indicating extraordinary psychic ability. Very rare.

Soothsayer - ancient word for a person doing psychic readings (from the word "sooth" meaning "truth"). The soothsayer is the person who tells a person the truth, whether it is something that he does not know; something that he knows but is overlooking; or something he knows that he needs independent confirmation of.

Square – square marking. Indicates protection.

Star - markings consisting of more than two overlapping lines forming an asterix. (Please note: the term "star" does not include a five pointed star or pentagram in this context). Stands for extraordinary events.

Tassel - a fork with many branches. In most areas, indicates divided energies.

Triangle – triangular mark. Indicates gifts from the Universe

Index

Catherine Kane is a professional psychic, Reiki Master/teacher, bard, artist, wordsmith and songwright, enthusiastic Student of the Universe, maker of very bad puns, and overachiever (amongst other things...)

She loves empowering people to find and live their best and brightest dreams. Palmistry is one of the ways that she does this.

Currently, Catherine is happily at work on her next book on surviving and thriving as a psychic empath, as well as upgrading her online course on palmistry.

Visit Catherine and her husband Starwolf as Foresight at www.ForesightYourPsychic.com,

www.ForesightYourCtPsychic.wordpress.com,

 Or on Face book at www.facebook.com/pages/Foresight/172408108291

Lightning Source UK Ltd.
Milton Keynes UK
UKHW011907050420
361356UK00001B/64